HIDDEN
HISTORY
of
YAKIMA

Ellen Allmendinger

History
PRESS

Published by The History Press
Charleston, SC
www.historypress.com

Front cover: Yakima Memory, a joint project of the Yakima Valley Museum and Yakima Valley Libraries.
Back cover: Yakima Memory, a joint project of the Yakima Valley Museum and Yakima Valley Libraries; *inset*: Justin Monwai.

Unless otherwise noted, images are courtesy of Yakima Memory, a joint project of the Yakima Valley Museum and Yakima Valley Libraries.

First published 2018

Manufactured in the United States

ISBN 9781467138413

Library of Congress Control Number: 2018945798

CONTENTS

Contents

ACKNOWLEDGEMENTS

This book is dedicated to the history lovers out there, particularly those in the Yakima Valley who have taken and supported the Yakima area historical walking tours. This book is truly a result of the success of the tours, which would not have been possible without those who attended the tours and shared information along the way.

It would be impossible to list everyone deserving credit for their support and assistance with this book. However, some very special people and organizations do deserve recognition.

A million thanks to my son Zakary and husband, Steve, for allowing me to lock myself away in archives, libraries and elsewhere to research and write. A huge thanks to my parents and other family members for their support, especially my mother, Mary, for her continual encouragement and assistance.

A huge thanks to Tammy Ayer and the *Yakima Herald Republic* for their support of the downtown Yakima tours, wonderful articles and information; Patti Hirahara for sharing her family story, support and historical information; the Inaba family and the Yakima Valley Japanese Community for sharing their stories, history and information; the On Chin, Mon Wai and Eddie Huie families for their stories, patience and explanations of the Chinese influence in Yakima; John Baule and the Yakima Valley Museum for answering so many questions, supplying so much historical information, allowing access to the archives and supporting the tours; Terry Walker and the various Yakima Valley Libraries for access to their wonderful archives and countless information; and Carla Adams and the Yakima Valley

Genealogical Society for their research assistance, support and patience as I spent countless hours at their wonderful library.

And I wish to thank, of course, all the wonderful people at The History Press and Arcadia Publishing for their patience and the opportunity to share some of Yakima's history.

INTRODUCTION

Today, very few clues remain of Yakima's intriguing and often forgotten past.

Although the railroad is the entire reason the city came into existence, the remaining historic passenger train depot provides few clues to the city's previous three passenger depots or to the historical events that occurred in or near it.

It's difficult to visualize the big circus acts that arrived in the city by train between the late 1890s and early 1900s. Imagining the crowds that gathered on Front Street to enter the circus tents or watch the acts at the intersection of Front Street and East Yakima Avenue is nearly impossible. Nor does it seem possible that their visits sometimes included deaths, arrests and legal issues.

Hidden in time is the reaction of the city's citizens and law enforcement agents when a woman wearing pants arrived in the city on the train. No women today could imagine being arrested for wearing pants.

Some of the oldest buildings in the city still stand across Front Street from the existing passenger train depot. The people who built and owned them, as well as those who conducted business from within their walls, have left few to no clues and have been forgotten over time.

Vanished is the city's once thriving China Town, which began with the city and lasted approximately seventy years. Of the almost four blocks that it dominated, today, only one business remains. The others are forgotten and remain hidden from site.

The city's Japan Town, which began in the early 1900s and grew to dominate a block by 1940, became nonexistent in 1942. Its buildings, businesses and people remain hidden from memory since the forcible evacuation and incarceration of those with Japanese heritage in the city.

Always hidden from site were the opium tunnels and dens that came into existence shortly after the city's beginning and were thought to be used by various people until possibly the 1980s. Today, only one entrance is thought to remain to the tunnels, the rest remain hidden from view.

Within the following pages one can discover some of the hidden and unseen histories of Yakima, its historical events, buildings and people.

PART I

FRONT STREET

In 1884, the Northern Pacific Railroad refused to place a passenger train depot at Yakima City (often called Old Town). Instead, it chose a barren, dusty, sagebrush-filled location approximately four miles to the north and filed a formal plat consisting of roads and numerous lots. It called its new plat North Yakima.

Only one problem remained. There were no people, buildings or businesses nearby for the railroad depot to serve. To remedy the problem, the railroad offered free lots to those in Old Town who chose to move their businesses to North Yakima. The result of the offer was an instant city with more than one hundred buildings moving from Old Town to North Yakima.

Front Street was one of the original streets on the formal plat; over the course of the next two years, it was filled with several of the original buildings that had moved to the new city. It was also the site of newly constructed ones. It was the first street those traveling by rail to the city encountered and the last for those departing on the train.

As time passed, new passenger depots were constructed, all of which faced Front Street. The significance and explanation for Front Street's impact on the city is primarily due to this proximity to the passenger depots as well as to the city's earliest businesses and buildings.

Today, Front Street is not as busy as it was a century ago. With the closure of the city's passenger train depots in the early 1980s and retail business issues, the street's lowest vehicle and pedestrian traffic occurred between the 1980s and the early 2000s. In the last decade, vehicle and foot traffic have increased, primarily due to the efforts of building and business owners within the Yakima North Front Street Historic District Association working to rejuvenate and restore the area.

Even with today's increase of travel on Front Street, much of this once important and highly traveled road remains hidden from memory. Forgotten are the first three passenger depots and the importance they once had. The overwhelming number of saloons and gambling halls that once lined the street—and the twenty-four-hour noise that created social issues—are not detectable or heard. The circuses that drew thousands of people to the vicinity also remain unimaginable.

The following chapters serve as a reminder of the importance and historic value of the once thriving Front Street.

NORTH YAKIMA'S
FOUR TRAIN DEPOTS

The first passenger train depot in North Yakima was nothing more than a wooden boxcar modified to operate as a depot and placed in the middle of Yakima Avenue. Remarkably, this small boxcar of a train depot was the beginning of a new city and nearly the demise of an already existing one. It was the entire reason that what was then North Yakima (now Yakima) even existed.

Placed in 1884, by the spring of 1885, the depot became the center of a lawsuit. Residents of Yakima City (Old Town), infuriated over the lack of a passenger depot, sued the railroad for refusing to build one in their city. The suit resulted in the railroad continuing to deny Old Town a new depot; it finally agreed to provide only a passenger stop there.

Within a year of formation, North Yakima grew rapidly, resulting in the boxcar passenger depot becoming obsolete and too small. To accommodate the rapid growth, the railroad built a second depot in 1886. Its location was near the first depot, blocking Yakima Avenue. The new depot was only slightly larger than the first, with a waiting area approximately ten feet by sixteen feet in size. It had one bathroom for both men and women. By 1887, Old Town, still unhappy about the lack of a passenger depot, sued the railroad once again.

Meanwhile, the second passenger train depot continued to operate and became the site of various incidents, some cheerful and some not. The most remembered was the Coxey Army Riot, which occurred in the spring of 1894 and ended with the shooting of two U.S. deputy marshals

Members of Coxey's Army at the second North Yakima passenger depot, May 1894.

and three Coxey's Army members. In total, an estimated 180 people were arrested and tried for the riot. It was an event few in the city cared to recall.

Over the next several years, the effectiveness of the second depot diminished. By 1896, the city's population had outgrown its size. To convince the railroad to build another depot, members of the Yakima Commercial Club traveled to Seattle in the spring of 1896 to meet with the general manager of Northern Pacific, who ultimately couldn't justify spending the estimated $6,000 to construct a new passenger depot. Discussion continued; by summer, an agreement that involved the railroad spending no new money on a depot was reached. Rather, the people of the city would pay for a depot and the maintenance of its grounds. This time, however, the third depot would be removed from the street, allowing east and west travel on Yakima Avenue. The plans were pleasing, although they wouldn't become reality for some time.

Two years later, there still was no new depot in the city. The second passenger depot was operating over capacity, with approximately thirty-five people fitting inside the waiting room and the remainder standing outside. Finally, Andrew Switzer was hired to construct a new passenger depot that

The third North Yakima passenger depot, view from Yakima Avenue.

would be more than one hundred feet long, more than thirty feet wide and one and a half stories high, with a forty-four-foot clock tower.

Andrew and his twelve-man crew started work on the third passenger depot in September 1898. Along the way, changes were made to the original plans, increasing the size of the new building and adding hookups for water and sewer lines. Costs were estimated to be $5,000, $1,000 less than the $6,000 budgeted two years earlier. The third passenger depot opened for operation in December 1898. Meanwhile, the second depot was removed from Yakima Avenue. The new depot was a huge improvement, with its concrete platform replacing the wooden one with splinters and spikes. The clock steeple was also appreciated and served citizens well, as did the Railway Park.

Although greatly improved, the third passenger depot lasted only about eight years before it would find itself in a state of deterioration. The city's population had continued to grow; once again, the depot was too small. Discussions regarding the building of yet another passenger depot ended abruptly in the spring of 1906, when a fire at the Pioneer Lumber Company spread to several businesses and destroyed the Northern Pacific Freight Depot. The passenger depot suffered some damages but was saved when a dozen freight cars were pulled between the fire and the depot.

The Railway Park located north of the third North Yakima passenger depot, circa 1908.

More than a year later, in July 1907, the assistant general passenger agent for the railroad, Mr. A. Charlton, declared the need for a new passenger depot in North Yakima. The following month, Mr. J. Deforce, the division superintendent of Northern Pacific, informed citizens that work on the new depot would begin in the spring of 1908. As in the past, spring came and went, and no new depot was constructed.

In 1908, the city was experiencing several health issues. Typhoid fever was spreading, city drinking water was declared unclean and the sanitary sewer conditions were viewed as deplorable. Along with other buildings in the city, the passenger depot was considered unsanitary. With no new passenger depot constructed, citizens began demanding that improvements be made.

Ira Englehart, an attorney for the railroad, finally announced in August 1908 that the railroad was considering building a new depot in the spring of 1909. Its cost was estimated to be between $75,000 and $100,000. By February 1909, a new estimate of $60,000 was announced. However, even with the reduction in price, no passenger depot was built in 1909.

Three years after initially being promised a new passenger depot, the city finally got one. It was built on the west side of North Front Street, directly across from A Street (now Sergeant Pendleton Way). Construction of the fourth and final passenger depot was completed in 1910. It still stands today, with many of its original features intact.

Passenger train service ended in the 1980s in Yakima, but the fourth passenger train depot has served as home to several businesses, including various offices, a brewery and restaurants. Today, it is the home to a coffeehouse and a restaurant.

2

SALOONS AND GAMBLING

North Yakima had an abundance of saloons, pool halls and gambling facilities when the city started. Saloons were so prevalent during the first years of the city's existence that they were one of the three main sources of activity. The number of saloons in the city far exceeded other businesses at the time. Some of the loudest noises consisted of music coming from saloons and the yelling of betting calls from gambling facilities. Noise wasn't the only issue; public drunkenness and crimes related to alcohol and gambling also escalated. The fact that the halls were open twenty-four hours a day didn't help matters.

Most saloons and gambling facilities in the early years were located on North or South Front Street, between A Street and East Walnut. One of the first was nothing more than a lean-to, eliminating the need for being indoors. By 1885, several indoor saloons existed, including the Board of Trade Saloon, Shardlow & McDaniel's Saloon, the Eureka Beer Hall, Dayton Beer and the Capital Saloon. Of these, the Board of Trade Saloon and Shardlow & McDaniel's Saloon became the most successful and operated in the city for years to come.

The Board of Trade Saloon was owned by Alvah Churchill. He was no stranger to running saloons, having operated one in Old Town since 1880. One of his employees in Old Town was Frank Shardlow. When Alvah relocated his saloon to North Yakima in 1885, Frank became his business partner. They opened their saloon on the northeast corner of Front Street and East Yakima Avenue, but their partnership didn't last long. The two

Men playing pool in a Front Street saloon.

went their own ways; Alvah remained the proprietor of the Board of Trade Saloon. (See chapter 8.) Frank opened a saloon on the south side of East Yakima Avenue for a brief period before leaving the city for a few years.

Frank Shardlow returned to the city in 1888. It didn't take long for Frank to find a new business partner—Jeff McDaniels—and open another saloon. Together, Frank and Jeff opened Shardlow & McDaniel's Saloon at the southeast corner of Front Street and East Yakima Avenue, directly across from Alvah's Board of Trade Saloon. The two saloons became competitors. Eventually, Jeff sold his portion of the saloon back to Frank. In 1902, Frank rebuilt the saloon and reopened it as Shardlow's Saloon; it became one of the more prominent saloons in the city.

Shardlow's Saloon also became a popular place to gamble and play billiards. Gambling would lead to one of the first armed robberies in the city. After a well-known gambling event, three armed men entered the saloon and robbed it. The thieves got away with money from the bar as well as from card dealers. Unfortunately, armed robbery wasn't the only negative gambling issue Frank's saloon would experience. His business was sued

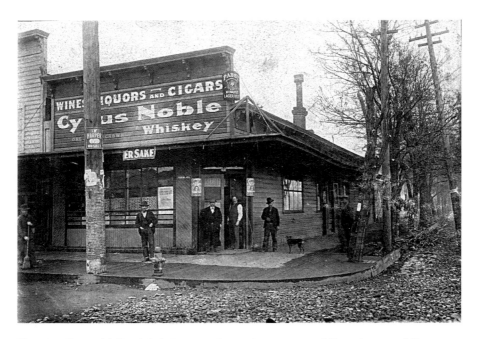

The Shardlow & McDaniel's Saloon, on the southeast corner of Front Street and East Yakima Avenue, circa 1890.

by the wife of a man who had allegedly gambled and lost all their money, leaving her poor and destitute. The suit, along with other gambling-related issues, resulted in city leaders placing a temporary ban on legal gambling. It wasn't the first or the last gambling ban the city experienced. Such bans were placed and then lifted depending on the time and the temperance of the citizens. When citizens became upset with gambling issues, bans were placed. When the taxes and permit money generated from the gambling facilities were missed and found to be beneficial, bans were lifted. Soon, restrictions on the sale of alcohol became an issue for the city.

Within four years of the city appearing on the map, most of the original saloons were closed. The city hadn't become drier, however. Rather, the closed saloons were replaced with others. In 1889, approximately one saloon was operating for every twenty businesses. The city's population expanded to approximately 3,154 people by 1905; the number of saloons increased as well.

Sixteen saloons were operating in the city in 1905, with approximately one saloon for every 197 people. Thirteen of the sixteen saloons were located on Front Street. They included the Byrnes & Tucker Saloon, Edward Van

Deist's Saloon, the F.E. Sherman Saloon, the Alfalfa Saloon, the Shardlow's Saloon, the C. Wilfong Saloon, Bert Fletchers' Saloon, the Rogers & Lee Saloon, the Heller & White Saloon, the Palace Bar, the J. Piland & Company Bar, Olaf Sandberg's Saloon and the John Steiner Saloon.

Saloons themselves weren't the only alcohol-related businesses in the city. In 1905, the North Yakima Brewing & Malting Company opened in the Switzer Opera House on North Front Street. It was the first brewery in the city, as well as one of the largest in the state. (See chapter 7.)

Citizens' concerns were rising regarding the increase in alcohol sales and consumption, not to mention the increased immoral behavior and criminal activity associated with it. Such behaviors kept the police department busy and the city jail full. Drunkards didn't have far to walk from the saloons on Front Street to behind bars in the city jail.

In the fall of 1905, city leaders passed an ordinance closing saloons—as well as other businesses—on Sundays. The intent of the ordinance was to provide for one day a week with no drinking or doing business in the city. The effect was marginal. Several men were arrested for conducting business. It didn't take long for people to realize that arresting business owners wasn't profitable; by January 1906, the city had repealed the ordinance. Saloons were back to serving on Sundays.

Outside social pressures occurring in the county were also impacting the decisions of authorities in the city when it came to the sale of alcohol. In 1907, Special Indian Agent Green traveled to North Yakima. After visiting, he declared the area to be the worst location for selling alcohol to Indians. As a result, Yakima County and North Yakima initiated a discriminatory decision forbidding the sale of alcohol to Native Americans. They threatened to stop renewing saloon licenses to those caught doing so, as well as fines or imprisonment if caught.

Regardless of the fines and restrictive laws, crimes related to alcohol continued to rise, as did the number of saloons in the city. By 1908, there were twenty-three saloons operating, twelve still located on Front Street. Opposition to saloons hadn't decreased, either.

Mr. Henry H. Wende was one such individual. He desired to once again make it illegal for saloons to be open on Sundays. Interestingly, per state law, it was already illegal, and the city for some reason had been overlooking this noncompliance. With Wende's reminder, the city once again began enforcing the Sunday saloon closure; those caught were fined or refused the renewal of their license. But it didn't slow down the business or prevent sales of alcohol on Sundays.

In July 1908, the owner of the Palace Saloon on Front Street was caught selling a bottle of beer on a Sunday. The city council, under the recommendation of the police committee, decided to punish the owner by not renewing or issuing a new saloon license. However, the punishment didn't last long. He was running his saloon a year later. Meanwhile, other trials for trafficking alcohol on Sundays occurred.

The rising cost of trials relating to alcohol found the city overwhelmed and farmers irritated. Farmers were paying most of the taxes to cover the court costs for saloon- and alcohol-related issues. They felt that the saloons themselves should be taxed more to cover such costs. It was a justifiable argument that led to the increase of fees.

In the summer of 1908, the National Issue League was also upset. Led by Dr. Grandville Lowther, the league gathered the signatures of citizens against saloons. When done, he presented the city council with a forty-foot-long petition containing two thousand names of those wanting saloons closed permanently.

North Yakima mayor Henry Lombard responded by proposing an ordinance that would allow one saloon per every thousand residents. His projection for the existing population of the city was fifteen thousand people, which would call for the closure of eight existing saloons. His proposal was dropped when the city council was hesitant to cut the taxes generated from eight saloons.

In January 1909, a compromise was finally reached. The city set the limit of saloons to twenty-two until the population reached twenty-two thousand people. In other words, there was no change to the existing number of saloons. However, Yakima County had adopted a new code that required saloons to install screens and obstructions over windows and doors to block the view of their interiors. The city also applied this code to the saloons.

Nine months later, City Councilman Andrew Jackson Shaw proposed the elimination of saloons on Yakima Avenue. He suggested the nonrenewal of licenses as well as forcing saloon owners to relocate their bars to the backs of their buildings. Five saloons were due to receive their renewals at the meeting, and Councilman Shaw's proposal did not pass. Rather, the council referred the decision to the police commission.

In October 1909, citizens finally petitioned to have an official anti-saloon vote taken to make North Yakima a dry city. On December 30, 1909, a formal vote occurred, with the outcome of 1,149 votes for saloons and 878 against them. North Yakima would not become a dry city—at least not yet. However, troubles continued for the saloons.

The State of Washington conducted an audit of saloons in the city and county in the spring of 1910. It discovered that the city, the county and saloons had not paid the state thousands of dollars in taxes. It also found several saloons and cigar stores operating without a license. Although unpaid state taxes were not taken lightly, it wasn't enough to close the saloons.

Issues surrounding saloons continued for almost six years until the State of Washington officially became dry in 1916. Sixteen saloons were operating in the city when Prohibition struck, and the city lost approximately $16,000 in saloon-related licenses and taxes. The buildings that once housed the saloons remained. Several gambling facilities simply turned into dry pool halls, while other vacated saloons were filled with non-alcohol-related businesses.

3
CIRCUS CONFUSION

Between the late 1890s and early 1900s, the arrival of various circuses in the city was frequent. Some years, the city was visited by multiple big-name shows, such as Robinson's Circus and Wallace's Circus in 1890. Other years, only one show rolled into town, like Sell's Circus in 1891. The big shows were a hit in the city and eagerly anticipated by citizens.

Unfortunately, not all circuses that came to the city left a pleasant taste for entertainment. When the Walter Main Circus arrived in July 1897, it took thirty-five train cars to transport the circus. It was greeted by many on Front Street as the equipment was unloaded. More would also crowd Front Street when the shows were put on. However, soon after the circus's departure, many were irritated. It had shorted the city $150 for its license to operate and overcharged people to attend.

Two years later, in 1899, Ringling Brothers Circus arrived. To help boost sales, the railroad promoted the event by offering a special fair on trains from nearby locations. High-wire acts had become popular, and the Ringling Brothers act featured Mr. H. Dubelle. The show turned out to be rather exciting, especially when seventeen people were arrested the day the circus held its show.

August 1903 brought the Campbell Brothers Circus to the city. It had a high-wire act as well. Unfortunately, it was not as successful as the Ringling Brothers Circus had been a few years earlier. After setting up tents in the middle of Front Street at East Yakima Avenue, Orin Butten began performing his high-wire act. He fell from the ceiling of the tent and died from a crushed skull. The tragic incident was widely reported.

Mr. Dubelle's high-wire act at the Front Street and East Yakima Avenue intersection, early 1900s.

In 1904, the Ringling Brothers Circus returned to the city. Luckily, no major incidents were reported relating to the circus itself, nor were any citizens arrested, as had been the case in its previous visit.

The summer of 1905 was a busier year for circuses. In June, the Norris & Rowe Circus arrived with tamed animals and a hippodrome. In August, the Barnum Circus came to town with an excellent ring work show. In the fall, the Sell's Floto Circus included a specialized Japanese balance/contortionist act. No major issues were reported with the three circuses that year. However, the following year wasn't as well received.

In May 1906, the Norris & Rowe Circus returned to North Yakima for its second visit within a year. Its acts consisted of chariot races, trained wild beasts, camels, llamas, seals, clowns and acrobatic performances. While in the city, one of the circus roustabouts, John Meredith, fell off one of the train cars and died. A second circus death within a few years wasn't exactly what one would expect.

The Norris & Rowe Circus returned to North Yakima the following year. Although no deaths were experienced, the city found itself in the middle of

Ringling Brothers Circus unloading at the third North Yakima train depot, 1904.

a legal battle once the show arrived. The circus employees claimed they were not getting paid and filed a lawsuit against the circus's owners.

By 1908, issues with circuses in the city also became social issues for the citizens. Thousands of people from around Yakima Valley were reported to have attended the circuses in the past. The city considered raising the cost of circus permits from $100 a day to $250. The consideration upset some citizens, who felt the rise in cost would prevent circuses from coming to the city.

Meanwhile, when the circuses arrived, kids wouldn't stay in school. In early June 1908, forty-three students skipped high school to watch the circus parade. The North Yakima police chief picked up several of the youths.

Circuses continued coming to North Yakima on the train and performing in the center of the city. However, after the fairgrounds became operational, most of the shows relocated there, limiting Front Street's view of the circuses to loading and unloading of the trains.

4
NELL PICKERELL

Nell Pickerell was born in Illinois in 1882. She arrived in western Washington with her family when she was a young girl. As a child, Nell's life was not easy. Although she had a doting mother, her father was a drunk and an abusive circus worker.

When Nell was sixteen, she found herself in the center of a situation that was considered socially taboo at the time. After having an affair with a much older man, she became pregnant. Because she was young and single, her mother raised her child, and Nell was known as his aunt. With her child living with her mother, Nell spent the early 1900s traveling throughout the Northwest, returning to the Seattle/Tacoma area after having experienced various social issues regarding the unacceptable behavior of a woman and a variety of criminal activities at various locations.

Nell experienced a good number of these social issues as a result of the various forms of employment she held. Frequently finding work as a bartender, barber, farmhand and even cowboy, Nell would often draw adverse attention. Her choice of employment resulted in unwanted attention, but it wasn't her only problem.

Legal issues also plagued Nell. In western Washington, she was incarcerated for being associated with theft, gang relations and transporting single young girls across state lines. She was usually released from jail due to lack of evidence. In other cases, she ended up going to court, where the charges were dropped, also from lack of evidence.

In 1906, Nell gave birth to another child out of wedlock to a man twenty years her senior. Having a second child out of wedlock furthered Nell's troublesome social issues. Pregnancy outside of wedlock was still frowned upon. The whereabouts of the child and father following the birth are unknown.

Two years later, on Friday, March 13, 1908, Nell Pickerell arrived in the city on a train. Her arrival was noted because of the nice men's clothes she was wearing and her alias—Harry Allen. North Yakima's police chief Short was aware of Nell's reputation as well as her arrival in the city.

During the weekend, Chief Short received reports of Nell being involved in bar fights. He also received complaints about her clothes. On Monday, Short arrested Nell and placed her in the city jail. While she waited to make bail, Nell was questioned by Short. She admitted her identity and explained that she wore men's clothing because they were comfortable and looked better on her than did dresses.

After Nell's bail was posted, she was released from jail. But she wasn't entirely free. She was escorted across North Front Street to the passenger train depot and told to leave the city. Leave she did, but not for long.

The following spring, in March 1909, Nell returned to North Yakima dressed as a man. She was recognized immediately. She broke no laws, but authorities weren't willing to allow her to stay in the city. They gave her three hours to leave. Nell obliged and left North Yakima, although she continued to travel in the Pacific Northwest.

In September 1916, Nell was stabbed by her father. She received injuries severe enough to almost kill her. She survived and lived for another six years. Sadly, Nell contracted syphilitic meningitis and died in December 1922. Her days of finding herself in the center of unfortunate social issues based on pregnancies, clothing choices and forms of employment were over.

PART II

OLD NORTH YAKIMA HISTORIC DISTRICT

Perhaps the most prominent historic block in the city lies within the border of North Front Street, East Yakima Avenue, North First Street and A Street (now Sergeant Pendleton Way). Today, most of this block is recognized as a historic district. The block was among the first to have its lots filled with buildings and businesses after the formation of North Yakima. It was also the first business block seen by those arriving in the city on the train, making the success of the businesses substantial in the city's early history.

Buildings that occupied this area were initially wood and consisted of saloons, stores, restaurants, hotels and lodging houses. Over time, the wood structures were replaced with more permanent brick-and-mortar buildings—a result of fires, social issues, age and, of course, money. The businesses within them continued to thrive, with the addition of hotels, municipal buildings, theaters and various offices.

Several of the buildings erected within the first two decades of the city's existence still stand on the block. In the last century, they have changed in appearance as well as in the businesses they house. Yet the history of the buildings and the businesses they once held remain hidden in the archives of history.

Other buildings have sadly been demolished for more than half a century. Their losses were a result of several issues, including parking and fire and safety reasons. Today, some of the lots now serve as parking lots or hold newer buildings, concealing what once stood.

The vitality and economic success of the block declined over time; the 1970s through approximately the early 1990s served as the area's least-frequented era. With the decrease in train travel, the increase in automobile travel and the expansion of the city, the popularity of the vicinity declined. Passenger train travel ended in the 1980s, making the area even less noticeable and helping to account for its once frequent reference as a red-light district. It was a hidden gem that just needed some time, attention and polishing.

In the last two decades, the block has regained popularity through the efforts of building and business owners. The Yakima North Front Street Historic District Association of Yakima—made up of property and business owners on the block—as well as members of the Yakima Historic Preservation Commission, Yakima Valley Historical Society and Downtown Association of Yakima have worked hard to recognize, preserve, rejuvenate and publicize their buildings and businesses as well as their historic significance in the city.

Today, the area is becoming more vibrant, appreciated and frequented by citizens and visitors alike. Sadly, the history of the buildings and businesses, as well as the people who ran them, often remain hidden within the walls of the existing buildings and out of sight from those seeing the parking lots now located there. The following chapters cover some of the buildings located on the block and help to reveal what remains hidden of their history and importance to the city.

THE SYDNEY HOTEL

One of the first businesses located at the southeast corner of Front Street and what was then A Street was the Fawcett Brothers Company. The firm operated from this location for several years, selling items such as seeds, farm implements, buggies and wagons. The store was well received and frequented in the city, so much so that it relocated to the northwest corner lot of East Yakima Avenue and North First Street in 1889. With the vacancy of Fawcett Brothers Company from its first location, the lot continued to serve as the site of several other businesses until 1909, when its new owner would pay for the construction of the building that remains standing today.

Julia Hess was a widow when she owned the West Side Boarding House on West Yakima Avenue, just west of the railroad tracks. In 1908, the North Coast Railway began condemning properties adjacent to the rails to obtain right-of-way. Julia lost her lodging house because of the condemnations, but she received $16,554.60 for her property. Having business experience, Julia used the money she received for her next investment property and business venture on the opposite side of the tracks.

In January 1909, Julia purchased the two lots on the southeast corner of North Front and A Streets, where Fawcett Brothers Company originally stood. She purchased the lots from Chris Christianson and his wife, to whom she paid $17,000. It was one of the highest-paid prices for property on North Front Street in the city's history. Upon purchase, Julia prepared to build a three-story hotel that she would call the Sydney Hotel. As expected with construction, issues occurred to slow the process.

The first issue involved a survey that indicated the city hall was encroaching onto her property by eleven inches. To resolve the situation without removing the city hall building, Julia requested that she attach her new building to the north wall of city hall. After review, the city agreed to her proposal rather than lose its municipal building. Today, the eleven-inch difference can be seen when standing at the connection of the two buildings.

In July 1909, Julia signed a contract with a builder to have the Sydney Hotel constructed. It was to be completed by January 1, 1910. However, it wasn't completed by the date agreed upon, and the contractor didn't use the materials she had specified and paid for. As a result, in May 1910, Julia filed a claim against the contractor for $13,704.54, which included the loss of hotel income.

The Sydney Hotel was finally opened for business later that year. Its location directly across North Front Street from the passenger train depot helped to establish it as the most convenient hotel in the city. The upper two floors served as the hotel, and the main floor was the location of the Sydney Saloon, the Sydney Café and the Sydney Cigar Stand. Of these three businesses, two would begin with problems.

In February 1910, before the hotel was in operation, an application for a retail liquor license for the Sydney Saloon was received by the City of North Yakima. The application ran into issues at a North Yakima City Council meeting when only one of the councilmen supported approval of the license. Other city council members, as well as other saloon owners, didn't want another saloon in the city. It took three city council meetings for the Sydney Saloon's liquor application to be approved.

Meanwhile, the Sydney Cigar Stand, which also sold fruits and sundries, couldn't keep the same owner for long. In April 1910, Mr. E. Morton owned the cigar store. By November, James Chisholm had purchased it. In the spring of 1911, Guy Allen purchased it. Within a month, he was trying to sell it. Cigar businesses were not the only issue the hotel had in 1911.

In November 1911, a wanted felon named George Pappas arrived in the city from Walla Walla, Washington. Law enforcement was warned of his arrival and greeted him at the train depot. While being escorted to the jail, he ran into the Sydney Hotel in an attempt to flee the officers. One officer fired two shots at the felon, missing his target and hitting a bystander in the arm instead. Pappas hid in a closet on the top floor until the officers found him.

Luckily, things weren't always so chaotic for the hotel. It operated successfully for decades under the care of various building owners and

Postcard of Sydney Hotel, located at the southeast corner of North Front and A Streets.

businesses. At some point, Julia Hess married and became Julia Hess Miller and eventually sold the building. She died in 1936 and is buried in Calvary Cemetery in Yakima.

Over time, the hotel changed names under other building and business ownership. The building's outside appearance changed as well. It was painted white for some time and then repainted other colors. The entrances and windows of the retail spaces on the main floor have also changed several times over the years, as have the businesses they housed.

Today, the building still stands at the corner lot within the Yakima North Front Street Historic District. Its upper floors currently serve as apartments, and the main floor has retail spaces.

6

THE NORTH YAKIMA CITY HALL, POLICE DEPARTMENT, CITY JAIL AND FIRE DEPARTMENT

During the first year of North Yakima's existence, no formal municipal government existed. Citizens held a meeting in the fall of 1885 and assigned Judge Carroll B. Graves and Edward Whitson the task of forming a suitable city government. The following January, North Yakima became an incorporated city with various leadership positions, offices and duties established. The first election was held in May 1888. With a government in place, it still had no municipal buildings to operate from.

The decision to erect a municipal building took nearly a year, with the major issue being the city not owning a lot to build on. The city was offered property, but it declined the offer. Instead, it purchased a lot for $5,990 from Andrew Switzer on the east side of North Front Street, between East Yakima Avenue and A Street. Afterward, it hired Andrew to erect a two-story, thirty-foot-wide and eighty-foot-long brick building. Switzer was paid $10,000 to erect the building. However, it's unclear if the $10,000 included the cost of the lot.

The North Yakima City Hall Building was completed in 1889. It housed the various municipal offices and departments, including the North Yakima City Council Office, North Yakima City Clerk's Office, North Yakima City Engineers Office, North Yakima Fire Department, North Yakima Police Department and the North Yakima City Jail. Upon completion and occupancy, the building was already full. It would amazingly act as a safety barrier the following spring.

In May 1890, one of the city's worst fires damaged or destroyed most of the wood buildings on North Front Street between East Yakima Avenue and the city hall. The new building prevented the fire from spreading farther north up North Front Street.

Over the next few years, finances were tight for the city, especially the fire department. In 1893, the department had some permanent paid employees, but most were men and women who volunteered for a bucket brigade. Safety attire for the firefighters was unavailable until people urged the city to purchase rubber suits. Once purchased, keeping them organized among the volunteers also became an issue.

The police department and the city jail were also struggling. There was a lack of space to effectively run the departments. Both were located at the east end of a hallway that passed the fire department's equipment and horse stalls. Office and locker spaces for the police department were small and awkward, as were the jail cells. The cells consisted of small spaces for dangerous criminals, one larger cell for men and one for women. No privacy existed between the male and female cells, which were overcrowded and considered unsanitary. They also weren't as secure as planned. In September 1900, a gas pipe was given to some of the prisoners, resulting in twelve inmates escaping. It wasn't the only time escapes occurred. In fact, they were frequent enough to be reported as far away as San Francisco.

North Yakima City Hall, Fire Department, Police Department and City Jail, approximately 1889.

In the spring of 1904, the fire department was experiencing more issues. The entire department went on strike to protest the lack of funding for safety equipment. It resulted in a reorganization of the department and a new chief and driver. The following year, there were demands that the city have a permanent, paid fire department. However, only three new employees were hired that fall: a chief and two associates. It took until the fall of 1907 for the fire department to see an increase in paid employees, expanding from four paid firefighters to fifteen.

First motorized fire engine in North Yakima, in front of the fire station located in the North Yakima City Hall on North Front Street.

The police department was also experiencing employee issues in 1907, including their authority to arrest people. By November, the department was half the size of earlier years and the jail was still overcrowded. Meanwhile, the department laid off three officers; only two officers were left on duty during the day shift and two on the night shift. Officer behavior was also becoming a concern to the citizens.

In the fall of 1908, citizens petitioned to have the police chief removed from the North Yakima Police Department when he reported that the youth of the city were behaving badly and he was involved in an incident reporting a minor in the jail. There was another reported incident involving a minor in the jail. The police committee investigated the conduct of the police chief in question as well as the North Yakima Police Department. Afterward, the police committee recommended that the mayor fire the police chief and also suspend an additional patrolman for violation of department rules.

A shakeup of the police department could not have come at a worse time in the city. North Yakima was continuing to grow in population.

The city hall after renovations, with various City of Yakima offices located within.

With the population rise came social issues and an increase in crime. Total arrests made in 1908 by the police department were reported as 1,559. If accurate—and assuming that number reflects the arrest of separate people—approximately 11 percent of the population was arrested. The overcrowded jails and large number of arrests led to the decision to hold only those arrested for serious crimes in the jail; the others were to be suspended.

The conditions at North Yakima City Hall were regarded as deplorable, filthy, smelly and unsanitary. Working conditions for employees in the fire and police departments weren't any better. The fire department had only eleven paid employees who were working twenty-one-hour shifts, six days a week. The police department employees were working twelve-hour shifts with a limited number of officers. Labor representatives finally stepped in; shifts were cut back to eight hours.

After years of problems, city leaders held meetings in 1911 regarding the relocation of the various municipal departments. It was agreed that new buildings were needed to house the offices. Future locations became an issue when the prices of lots were discussed. Locations of lots were finally agreed upon and purchased, and buildings were erected.

With the new buildings completed, the departments vacated the old city hall. Discussions were then held to destroy the building due to its deteriorating condition. Instead, the interior of the structure was remodeled.

Following renovations to the building, some of the city offices returned. They remained in the building for some time. Here, citizens could receive polio shots, purchase dog permits and obtain bicycle licenses.

Eventually, city offices moved out; the building never served as a city municipal location again. In the 1980s, it became part of Grant's Pub & Brewery. Later, it was home to another bar.

Today, the Old City Hall Building stands as the second-oldest structure in the city. Its current owner has modified the upper floors into living space; the bottom floor holds a hair salon.

7

THE SWITZER OPERA HOUSE

Andrew Switzer was born in Maryland in March 1845. By 1880, he and his wife, Emma, who was born in Michigan, had made their way to Oregon with their son. While in Oregon, the couple had a daughter. Before 1883, Andrew, Emma and their young daughter left Oregon, leaving their son behind, and headed north to the Yakima Valley. A carpenter by trade, Andrew become one of the early well-known builders in the area. He was responsible for erecting many of the buildings in the city, several of which still stand, such as the old city hall, the Switzer Opera House and the Lund Building. However, it is for the opera house, located on the east side of North Front Street, midblock between East Yakima Avenue and what was then A Street, that he is most remembered.

Confusion often exists regarding the North Yakima City Hall and the Switzer Opera House buildings. The two are often mistaken as the same building when, in fact, they are separate buildings. Andrew Switzer completed the city hall first and then constructed the opera house.

For its day and for the size of the city, the Switzer Opera House was considered large, seating more than three hundred people. It was also popular. Traveling opera productions, bands and other shows often performed within its walls. However, it wasn't only operas and traveling shows that drew people to the building. Large conventions, balls and meetings were also held there.

In May 1893, the Yakima County Republican Convention was held in North Yakima. Included as part of the convention was a centennial celebration. The Switzer Opera House was one of the locations where the festivities were held. A few months later, in July 1893, the State Industrial Convention was held in the city. Part of that convention, hosted by the Farmers' Alliance, the Knights of Labor and Good Templars, took place in the opera house.

Meetings of local military and cavalry troops were also held in the building over the years. Events such as the North Yakima Fire Department's fundraising balls, various school balls and dances, as well as other sponsored events occurred. The Washington State and Yakima County Beekeepers Associations held regular meetings in the opera house, as did other agricultural associations and groups.

Within a decade of the Switzer Opera House's opening, the Mason Opera House on East Yakima Avenue opened. Over time, the Mason Opera House

The North Yakima City Hall (*left*) and Switzer's Opera House (*right*) in 1900. Both buildings were constructed at separate times by Andrew Switzer.

became more popular; within a few years, Andrew closed the doors to his opera house. Sadly, closing his business wouldn't be the only loss in Andrew's life in the beginning of the 1900s.

Andrews's wife, Emma, had returned home to Flint, Michigan, with their daughter. It was there that she died in March 1902. Andrew traveled to Michigan to claim his wife's body, but he didn't stay long. He returned to the city alone as a widower by 1903 and was living in the Stone Hotel on North Front Street. By 1910, he had relocated to Seattle, Washington, ending his time spent living and working as a builder in North Yakima. The building did not disappear after he left the city. Rather, it remained standing and soon became the location of a completely different business.

In the fall of 1904, the North Yakima Brewing & Malting Company purchased the Switzer Opera House building. The company had four partners at the time of purchase: brothers John Schlotfeldt and Herman Schlotfeldt, John P. Clerf and C.R. Oppenlander. The Schlotfeldt brothers were already business owners in the state. John owned the Roslyn Brewing & Malting Company in Roslyn, Washington, and Herman ran the Schlotfeldt Brothers Company in Port Townsend, Washington. Both brothers resided in Ellensburg at the time of the Switzer Opera House purchase. John Clerf was also residing in Ellensburg, while the fourth partner, C.R. Oppenlander, lived in Roslyn at the time.

After purchasing the building, the partners spent $40,000 remodeling to accommodate their brewery. The projected capacity of output was two thousand barrels a day. To meet the expected quantities, they built an addition on the back of the building. Work was completed approximately one year later. When it opened, it was one of, if not the biggest, breweries in the state.

The North Yakima Brewing & Malting Company was prosperous, but it did experience a few hitches along the way. It employed both union and nonunion workers at the brewery; soon, the length of the workday became an issue. To resolve the issue, a union whistle was installed to go off at 5:00 a.m. and 5:00 p.m., indicating the beginning and end of an eight-hour shift.

In 1908, the company purchased the Sinclair Ice Company in North Yakima for $10,000. It intended to spend another $50,000 modifying the ice company's building into a malting and bottling plant. The partners also planned on investing $40,000 on business improvements and expansions. However, all plans for the North Yakima Brewing & Malting Company's expansions halted in February 1908 with the threat of the city going dry.

The city did not go dry in 1908, and business for the brewery continued to be successful. In 1909, it added a corrugated iron building to the back of the opera house to use as a storage area for its beer. This was a necessary addition, considering the firm was shipping beer to various locations away from the city and was supplying between one-half and three-quarters of the saloons in the city with beer.

In 1910, the threat of prohibition was still a problem for the brewery. Temperaments were rising in the city. John Schlotfeldt became engaged in an argument on Front Street with Dr. Morton Rose, a reverend from the First Christian Church. The argument concerned conditions in Pendleton, Oregon, after it went dry. John believed that Pendleton was suffering in the wake of going dry, while the reverend believed differently. A crowd of bystanders witnessed their argument; finally, it was agreed that the two would travel together to Pendleton to assess who was correct. When they returned, John admitted that his dire story of the city suffering was perhaps not entirely true.

The North Yakima Brewing & Malting Company continued to operate; by 1911, it managed to have a monopoly on the sale of beer in the city. In October, Mayor Andrew Splawn declared that outside breweries in Seattle and Tacoma shouldn't be allowed to sell their product in North Yakima and only those breweries existing in the city should have products sold in the city's saloons.

Three years later, with continuing threats of prohibition, other breweries in the state were considering relocating to California. The owners of the North Yakima Brewing & Malting Company were planning on staying in business until prohibition occurred and then converting their business into a fruit by-products company. Their theory was that thousands of tons of fruit were going to waste in the valley. They planned on purchasing the fruit and producing grape juice, canned and evaporated fruit, vinegar and other products. It was a great plan in theory, but it never came to fruition.

On January 1, 1916, when prohibition became law, the brewery had not switched to a fruit by-products plant. Instead, it closed. With the company's departure from the building, other activities and businesses would soon fill the space. In 1919, the building served as a location for the gathering, staging and sorting of various goods to be shipped overseas. The operation was part of a World War I relief program.

The building also had new owners in 1919. J.J. Crawford and W.E. Norton purchased the building and opened the Yakima Transfer & Storage Company. They ran their business from the building until 1948, when they sold to Lon Robinson. A few years later, Robinson sold the business to Elwood Miller, who continued to run it from the building until 1976. Afterward, the building returned to the brewery business.

Goods sorted in the Switzer Opera House for the overseas relief project during World War I.

In 1982, Herbert Bert Grant, a Scottish-born brewer, opened a brewery in the Switzer Opera House building. He named his company the Yakima Brewing & Malting Company, but it also became known as Grant's Pub & Brewery. It is believed that his brewery was one of the first of its kind to open after prohibition ended. Grant ran his business from the Switzer Opera House building before expanding into the old city hall and then across North Front Street to the fourth passenger train depot.

Since Grant's Pub & Brewery left the Switzer Opera House, other businesses have taken up residence there. They include a restaurant, retail stores and another brewery. During this time, the building also had an owner who wished to see it rejuvenated and its historical value appreciated.

In 2017, the building was sold once again. Its current owner hopes to continue renovating the building and preserving its historical value.

8

THE LUND BUILDING

Alvah Churchill was born in Iowa around 1843. Prior to 1880, he had made his way west and married his wife, Amanda (Goodwin) Churchill. He was operating a saloon in Old Town, but when businesses were offered free lots to relocate to North Yakima, Alvah joined the move and relocated his saloon.

In 1885, with the help of an employee and new business partner, Frank Shardlow, Alvah opened the Board of Trade Saloon on the northeast corner of East Yakima Avenue and Front Street. Its location directly across the street from the first passenger train depot allowed the saloon to be highly visible. The business partnership of Alvah and Frank ended shortly after the relocation of the saloon. Alvah became the saloon's sole proprietor. (See chapter 2.)

Alvah ran the Board of Trade Saloon for another five years until a fire devastated the building in May 1890. The building was destroyed, leaving Alvah with $9,000 in damages, $3,000 of which was covered by insurance. Suffering from ill health, Alvah was done with the saloon business. On January 7, 1891, he passed away at the age of forty-seven in Portland, Oregon, where he had traveled to receive medical help. He was survived by his wife, Amanda, and seven children. The lot where Alvah's saloon once stood was now for sale. It didn't take long for it to be purchased by a new owner.

Born in Mandell, Norway, in 1855, Thomas Lund was originally a seaman, at one time clinging for life to the mast of a ship. Later, he became a merchant ship captain. Thomas immigrated to the United States around 1875 and returned to working on the water by becoming a pilot on a ship on the Columbia River. He eventually relocated to Tacoma, Washington, and then to Roslyn, Washington, where he worked as a merchant and a saloonkeeper. The latter was a profession he would carry with him to North Yakima.

Prior to December 1893, Thomas became the next owner of Alvah Churchill's old lot. He had another wood building erected after the fire and opened the Alfalfa Saloon. Meanwhile, Thomas made plans for improvements to the building. He hired Andrew Switzer to construct a new building at the cost of $4,000. The building included a basement as well as living quarters on the second floor. On its completion in 1898, Thomas moved into the upstairs section to live and opened the Alfalfa Saloon on the main floor. A few years later, he spent another $3,500 improving the building by adding on to the east and north sides.

Just prior to 1905, Sam Chong opened Sam's Café in the new east addition of the building. A well-liked Chinese business owner in the city, Sam ran his café from the location for fifteen years, closing it in 1920. (See chapter 12.)

Not long after Sam's Café opened, Thomas Lund's health began deteriorating. In 1905, his three nephews—Ernest, Alfred and Harold—managed the Alfalfa Saloon for him while he made his last trip back to Norway with his daughter Lena. He returned to the city and remained living on the second floor of the building while his nephews ran the saloon below.

On January 10, 1906, Thomas passed away in his upstairs room in the Lund Building. He died of rheumatoid heart issues, a health issue he claimed he had received while trying to survive the shipwreck years earlier. His nephews continued operating the saloon after his death until 1912, when it closed.

In 1914, a Mr. Joseph and Mrs. Applebaum, owners of a store named the Chicago Clothing Company, relocated their business to the Lund Building. They operated the store at this location until 1919, when they sold it to Sid and Charlie Neuman. The Neumans ran the clothing store until the 1940s, when they sold it to one of their longtime employees.

Al Egley was born on October 21, 1899. He arrived in North Yakima in 1903 with his parents. Around the age of fifteen, Al applied for, and secured, a job at the Chicago Clothing Company. He worked for the company as a valued employee until the early 1940s, when he purchased it from the Neumans.

The inside of the Alfalfa Saloon, located within the Lund Building, in 1898.

While the Chicago Clothing Company occupied part of the Lund Building, a well-liked tavern, the Shasta, resided in the east side of the building, where Sam's Café had operated decades earlier. In the 1950s, the Shasta served lunches and beverages, sold cigars and hosted billiards and card games.

Al Egley continued to own and operate the Chicago Clothing Company in the Lund Building until 1969, when he relocated the store to a different location on East Yakima Avenue. It would be more than a decade before another prominent store would last in the location. In the 1970s, the building was in what was known as the red-light district.

In the early 1980s, the building's owners were Dr. Robert and Peggy Henretig, who had purchased it around 1981. In 1982, another popular clothing store leased a space from the Henretigs in the Lund Building. This time, however, it was a clothing store for women and was called Corday's Women's Clothier. The store operated from the location for approximately two decades before closing.

The Chicago Clothing Company and the Shasta Tavern inside the Lund Building in April 1957. (The Lund Building is shown on the left in what appears as two buildings but is actually one.) The buildings to the east of the Lund Building were the homes to Frank Nagler Cigar Company, Fred Mailloux Company (Roxy Theatre in photo) and H.H. Schott & Company (left side of the Washington Hotel).

In the 1980s, the owner of Corday's Women's Clothier purchased the Lund Building from the Henretigs and still owns it today. Although Corday's has closed, the building's owner has had the upstairs renovated into apartments and tries to retain the building's historical value.

Since the closing of Corday's, the building has been the location of various restaurants and wineries, including the Greystone Restaurant and 5 North. Today, a winery and another restaurant occupy the main floor of the building.

9

THE NAGLER CIGAR STORE

rank X. Nagler was born in Bavaria, Germany, in June 1867. As a child, he excelled in music, a trait he learned from his father, a military bandleader. By the age of sixteen, Frank had moved to Minnesota and was learning how to make cigars. Both music and the cigar-making trade would extend into his adulthood and become part of his future occupations.

After living in Minnesota for approximately three years, Frank moved to Ellensburg, Washington, where he established a cigar-manufacturing business with George Faltermeyer in 1866. He also started teaching music and leading a band. He was successful at both.

Around 1889, Frank relocated to North Yakima and opened another cigar-manufacturing business with George. They named their firm the Nagler & Faltermeyer Company. The first cigar-manufacturing company in the city, it was located on the north side of East Yakima Avenue, between Front and First Streets, one lot east of the Lund Building. In the building, they not only manufactured cigars but also sold them wholesale.

While running their cigar manufacturing company in North Yakima, the two still maintained their company in Ellensburg. In the fall of 1890, Frank returned to Ellensburg for a brief period to manage the store and lead a band. However, he returned to North Yakima in the spring of 1891, just in time for the two men to enter another partnership.

In 1891, Frank and George married sisters in a double wedding at St. Joseph's Catholic Church in North Yakima. Their new brides had been raised by the Catholic Sisters of Yakima after the death of their mother. After the weddings, Frank and George continued to operate as partners until

Frank Nagler Cigar Company (left), Fred Mailloux & Company Store and H.H. Schott & Company Building, 1905.

1895, when George retired and moved to Minnesota, leaving Frank as the sole owner of North Yakima's first cigar-manufacturing company.

Frank also had other business ventures in the area. He owned stock in mining and was the treasurer of the Elizabeth Gold Hill Mining Company, which was operating approximately seventy miles northwest of the city. Frank used his involvement in mining to lure customers into his cigar shop. In 1905, he had a special exhibit of an ore found at the Elizabeth Gold Mines displayed in his cigar store. The ore was reported to contain gold, silver, copper and lead, with a gold value of $88 a ton. Although the display was popular and brought people into the store, it was only temporary.

Music still played a large role in Frank's life, and he used it to bring people to his cigar store. In 1907, the first musicians union in the city was formed. Frank became a member, and the group held some of its meetings in his business.

After about nineteen years of running his cigar business, Frank decided to leave it and pursue music. In the spring of 1908, he sold his factory and retail business to J.F. Moore, also from Minnesota. With his brother, Moore continued to operate the cigar manufacturer and sales business under the name Moore Brothers.

Later, the building held several other businesses until the late 1950s, when it was slated to be demolished. At some point in the 1960s, the building was torn down. Today, it is the site of a parking lot immediately east of the Lund Building.

10

The Fred Mailloux & Company

The Mailloux family immigrated to the United States from French Canada around 1882. After making their way west, they arrived in North Yakima and opened a grocery store in the city.

The Fred Mailloux & Company store was located on the north side of East Yakima Avenue, between Front and First Streets, one building east of the Nagler Cigar Store. Owned by Fred and Eldege Mailloux, the store became the first grocery in the city to make free deliveries within the city limits. Later, it delivered goods outside the city limits using a horse and wagon to locations like Moxee, Washington.

Selling fine goods and fancy groceries, the Fred Mailloux & Company often advertised as paying the highest market prices for farm produce. It also took over grocery stock from other stores and added it to its line of goods. If its advertisements are to be believed, one of the reasons the company flourished was that it sold all the fine goods at the lowest prices in the city.

By the summer of 1900, the Maillouxs had decided to expand their business. Rather than relocating to a different building, they removed a dividing wall between their store and a tailor located in the building one lot east.

In 1905, the Maillouxs accepted only cash purchases at their store. They also began selling items other than groceries. Clothing, blankets and toilets were added to the stock at reduced prices. Their customers could buy their groceries, a pair of boy's blue overalls for $0.25 and a suit that was normally $9.00 for $4.99.

Fred and Eldege Mailloux before
arriving in North Yakima.

One thing not for sale in their store was a dog. The dog lived in the store and turned out to be a wonderful addition, not to mention a form of security. Robbers broke into the Fred Mailloux & Company store in 1907 and attempted to steal a till when the dog frightened them away. The thieves dropped the till and the key that they had used to gain access. The dog saved the business a reported $1,000 from the foiled robbery.

In the early 1900s, various businesses in the city would enter a friendly competition of decorating their stores for the fair season. Citizens would vote on the decors, and a winner would be decided. The Fred Mailloux & Company participated frequently in such events. In September 1907, it won for best decor. The store was decorated with a variety of fruits, vegetables, leaves and flowers extending from the ceiling and a 142-pound squash.

The Fred Mailloux & Company closed its doors for business sometime around 1930, leaving the building available for others. Fred passed away on April 24, 1937, and was buried in Calvary Cemetery.

The Roxy Theatre, once the site of Fred Mailloux & Company, 1938.

With the Maillouxs' store closing, the building was made available for other businesses. At some point in the 1930s, it became the location of one of the city's most remembered theaters, the Roxy Theatre. It operated from the location for the next few decades and served as the source of many memories for city residents.

By the late 1950s, it was decided that the building that housed the Roxy Theatre would be torn down for parking. It was demolished in the 1960s along with buildings immediately surrounding it. A parking lot and a drive-through fast-food restaurant now stand in its place.

The H.H. Schott & Company

Henry H. Schott left Minnesota around the age of twenty-one, arriving in North Yakima with his new bride, Mary Schott, in 1890. Upon their arrival, Henry opened the H.H. Schott & Company, also known as the Schott's Cash Company. The company was in the Rosenfeld Building, on the north side of East Yakima Avenue, just one lot west of the North First Street intersection.

His company was known for buying portions, or an entire stock, from companies closing their doors and selling secondhand goods. Customers could buy a variety of items at the company, including but not limited to shirts, corsets, umbrellas, china, holiday items and fabric.

Just prior to 1898, it was announced that the store would be remodeled and become a new store, the Golden Rule. Although this name was used in advertisements, the company also used "H.H. Schott & Company" in the same ads. The names of the H.H. Schott & Company as well as the Schott's Cash Company were painted on the building; the name of the Golden Rule was not.

In December 1900, Henry decided to further expand his business and building. To do so, he expanded into the alleyway and added a floor. The improvements were not small in nature, nor were they inexpensive. He traveled to Tacoma for many of the necessary supplies for the remodeling. By the fall of 1901, the H.H. Schott & Company building's remodel was complete. The improved, three-story brick building dominated the block in size at the time.

Postcard of the Henry H. Schott & Company Building, pre-1908.

Soon after opening in the new building, the store was robbed on a Saturday evening in September. The thieves made their escape with approximately $200 in one size of cloaks, shirtwaists and corsets. It was suspected that a Japanese gang had committed the robbery. With little proof, law officers somehow obtained a search warrant for the Japanese held in suspicion, but no proof was found as a result of searches.

In 1901, Henry leased out part of his large building to Mrs. E. Miller. She operated a millinery business from the location. Her store offered a wide variety of hats and other items such as camel and beaver materials and ostrich feathers. Her business did well, but it did not operate long at that location. By November 1902, she had held an inventory closing-out sale. The sale was presumably due to Henry selling his building and eventually his business and merchandise.

By February 1902, Henry Schott sold his building to A.E. Larson for $25,000. After the sale, Henry still operated the H.H. Scott & Company Store from the location. In an October 1902 advertisement, Henry announced that his store was going out of business and he was having a closing-out sale of $125,000 of stock. Later, he sold his remaining stock of merchandise to Stone, Fisher & Lane. The sale had some type of problem, however, and at

The old H.H. Schott & Company Building, incorporated as part of the Washington Hotel (*left side of photo*); Panama Hotel and Red Apple Café, Yakima Lodging and Empire Hotel (*right side of photo*), June 1916.

one point he threatened to sue Stone, Fisher & Lane for $50,000 over the sale of the merchandise.

After selling his building and stock, Henry became active in city politics. In 1907, he became a councilman at large for the City of North Yakima; in 1910, he became mayor. After leaving his building, it wasn't only his career that changed paths. His former building would also soon change.

In 1905, Patrick Mullins, a wealthy new property owner, purchased the building from A.E. Larson and the properties immediately to the east, on the northwest corner of East Yakima Avenue and First Street. It was Mullins's second big business purchase in the city and one that would soon earn him a place as the city's leading hotel man. (See chapter 18.)

Approximately two years after Patrick purchased the lots, at the end of 1907 and the beginning of 1908, he began building the Washington Hotel. Part of the new hotel construction incorporated the old Henry Schott building, as well as the addition of another floor. The incorporation into the Washington Hotel forever changed the outward façade of the building.

In December 1970, two fires started on the same day in the Washington Hotel. People living in the building were evacuated. Less than a week later, another fire started in the hotel. This time, it completely devastated the building, forcing its demolition.

Another building was erected at the site and was home to various restaurants. Today, the lots that once held the H.H. Schott & Company and the Washington Hotel are home to a parking lot and a drive-through fast-food restaurant.

PART III

CHINA TOWN

On May 6, 1882, President Chester Arthur signed into law the Chinese Exclusion Act as an attempt to appease and calm white protestors and labor unions. It was the first and only law of its kind in the country that prohibited the immigration of people based on a specific nationality. It helped the white labor movement but punished the Chinese already in the country. The act was initially slated to last ten years, but it was extended and modified in various forms until World War II and beyond.

With the Chinese Exclusion Act, those in China could no longer immigrate to America, particularly laborers. An exception was the allowance of Chinese already in the country to petition to bring their children still living in China. Sadly, this did not include wives of males already in the country. As a result, many families were living in America without the wives or mothers. If the children of those already living here arrived, the Chinese Exclusion Act prohibited them from becoming American citizens.

Prior to the signing of the act, Chinese immigrants were already living in Yakima County. Four years before North Yakima became a city, the 1880 Washington Territory Census indicated that thirty-two Chinese people were living in Yakima County. A decade later, fifty-three Chinese people were living in the city. As the city's population grew, so did the number of Chinese in North Yakima.

Most of the Chinese living in the city resided in various businesses, lodging houses or hotels within what would become known by locals as China Town. This section was roughly located between South Front Street, east to South Second Street and East Yakima Avenue south to East Walnut.

Although the area known as China Town was recognized by local citizens, law enforcement and newspapers, it was not as easily identified when walking down the street. The buildings that the Chinese lived and worked in were built and owned by whites. No visible decor on the outside of the buildings existed; most of the businesses had English signs and names.

Although there were no known anti-Chinese riots in the city or its China Town, the Chinese in North Yakima experienced plenty of anti-Chinese rhetoric and social issues. In 1895, Leigh Freeman, an editor and newspaper owner in the city, was strongly opposed to the hiring of Chinese people. Known for expressing his opinion on the streets, he used his position as a newspaper owner to publicly express anti-Chinese sentiment and to lament the lack of work for white people. (It's no coincidence that Leigh Freeman's son Miller would become the editor of newspapers in the Seattle area and one of the most recognizable anti-Japanese leaders in the state.)

By the early 1900s, several Chinese in North Yakima had become respected by many in the city, particularly those with restaurants. Sadly, the restaurants also became the source of anti-Asian contention for years.

The use of private dining boxes in Asian restaurants was common in the city. They were used for family, business gatherings and celebrations. However, the private boxes also served as a source of harassment from police officers and some city leaders. Their justifications for the harassment was their belief that the boxes were a source of immoral and illegal activities.

From 1908 to 1911, North Yakima police officers began arresting and fining Chinese restaurant owners over private boxes. City leaders signed an ordinance restricting the wall height of private boxes in Asian restaurants, even though police officers and others had testified in court that the boxes in question were visible to others in the establishment.

In 1908, Chinese and Japanese restaurant owners in the city became the center of false newspaper reports. Papers throughout the Northwest were reporting that the Chinese and Japanese were taking over all the restaurants in the city. Although false, the reports were successful in spreading fear and anger. They also resulted in white restaurant owners grouping together and refusing to hire Chinese employees, as well as not allowing them into their businesses.

As time passed and the population continued to grow in the city, so did the number of Chinese residents and businesses. In the early 1900s, Japanese immigrants began arriving in the city and opening businesses, most within one of the China Town blocks (between South Front Street, East Yakima Avenue, South First Street and East Walnut). The Chinese and Japanese worked alongside one another until the evacuation of the Japanese in 1942.

Yakima's China Town began in the 1890s and continued to grow through about the 1940s. New Chinese businesses stabilized from the 1930s to the '50s and then decreased as time passed. Although the businesses declined, many families still lived within hotels and buildings in the district through the 1980s.

12

SAM'S CAFÉ

S am Chong was one of North Yakima's most prominent Chinese business owners and a respected Chinese community leader. Born in China about 1864, Sam arrived in the country in 1884.

The Chong family arrived in North Yakima prior to 1905. Sam arrived with his wife, Uottai (Stella) Lee, who was born in Oregon in approximately 1884. In 1905, they had their first child, Albert. They also opened Sam's first of many businesses in the city.

Sam's Café opened in 1905. It was in the east side of the Lund Building on the corner of East Yakima Avenue and Front Street, across from the north border of the then China Town. (See chapter 8.) It was from this location that Sam successfully ran his café for the next fifteen years, although there were some legal, social and family issues along the way.

Like other Chinese restaurants in the city, Sam's Café had private boxes. In February 1908, North Yakima's mayor, Henry Lombard, insisted that all private enclosures in restaurants have walls no higher than three and a half feet. Because Sam was a successful businessman, he was able to hire Henry J. Snively as an attorney. On the advice of Henry, Sam, along with the owners of the Richelieu Restaurant, did not shorten the walls or remove the curtains from their private boxes.

A few months later, the private boxes in his restaurant would once again become an issue. In the spring of 1908, the city passed an ordinance to enforce the removal of private boxes, and Sam was fined. Henry Snively represented him in court and testified that his restaurant's boxes weren't as

Sam Chong.

private as charged and that those diners in the main eating room could see what was occurring inside of the boxes. A North Yakima policeman also testified that Sam's boxes were not private to the public's eye. Sam was found not guilty in court. Unfortunately, private boxes weren't the only social issue Sam would face that year.

Newspapers throughout the Northwest reported that the Chinese and Japanese in North Yakima were forming hashery trusts and attempting to take over all the restaurants in the city. Although there were several Asian-owned restaurants in the city, there were more non-Asian restaurants. Regardless, several of the white-owned restaurant owners began a campaign and refused to hire Asian employees.

A year later, the struggle with private boxes in restaurants remained an issue. Sam was still fighting for the right to maintain private boxes in his restaurant. He was once again fined ten dollars and the cost of police court for continuing to operate with them. Henry Snively was prepared to take the case to the Washington State Supreme Court to determine if the city ordinance was legal. The result of any supreme court case is unknown, but no subsequent mention of private boxes could be found.

In the early 1900s, amid all the controversy, Sam was considered a social and financial pillar in the city's Chinese community. He was often reported as buying tickets for poor Chinese who wanted to go back to China and hiring attorneys for Chinese who couldn't afford to do so themselves.

Of course, Sam was also a husband and a father. Although his business was on East Yakima Avenue, his family lived at 505 South First Street. By 1918, Sam and his wife had five sons. Tragically, two of his children died at their home within a week of one another. Their son Albert was thirteen years old when he passed away from pneumonia on October 17. Less than a week later, on October 23, their sixteen-month-old son Lester also died of pneumonia. Both sons were buried in a small Chinese section of Tahoma

Cemetery in a private ceremony. Meanwhile, their other children were also ill but recovered.

Sam would operate Sam's Café from the Lund Building for only two more years. After closing the café in 1920, the family continued to live on South First Street, but Sam turned his attention to farming in Toppenish, Washington. He farmed until 1923 and then turned his attention back to business in the city.

In 1923, Sam took over the Wing Chong Lung Company at 126 South First Street. In 1924, the store's name was changed to the Yuen Chong Company. It specialized in sales of Chinese merchandise and groceries. Little is known about the building from which Sam operated the Yuen Chong Company.

Six years later, in 1929, Sam was still running his store on South First Street. He also opened a cigar store, the Yuen Chong Cigar Company. It was located at 11 South Front Street, within the then thriving Japan Town. Sam's dual business ownership lasted until 1932, when he closed both stores.

Five years later, in 1937, Sam opened his last business in the city, one that would also become a family-run operation. The Sam Chong Cigars store opened on the south side of East Chestnut, between Front and First Streets. It was located within China Town, across East Chestnut from the Montana Hotel. While Sam was operating the cigar store, his wife, Stella, died at the age of fifty-nine on December 29, 1943. After Stella's death, Sam continued to operate the store and was soon joined by his son.

Andrew Chong was working at Boeing during World War II. After the war, in his thirties, he returned to Yakima and worked alongside his father at the cigar store. Together, father and son ran the business until Sam was in his nineties. They closed the Sam Chong Cigars store in 1956. Sadly, Sam died a few years later, in September 1959.

Andrew remained in the city with his own family after his father's death. He later created Chong Investments, a rental-property company. Before fully retiring, Andrew also worked at the Golden Wheel Restaurant. (See chapter 14.) He passed away in December 2001.

The Lund Building, out of which Sam operated Sam's Café, is still standing and has housed various business and restaurants since Sam's Café closed. (See chapter 8.) The building that held his last business, the Sam Chong Cigars store on East Chestnut, is no longer standing. The site now contains a parking lot.

13

THE RICHELIEU AND
NEW RICHMOND CAFÉ

Within five years of North Yakima's formation, several members of the Wong family had already immigrated to the country from China and arrived in the city. Family members continued to come to the city over the next four decades and became well known for their culinary skills.

Lucy Wong was one of those family members who became known for their cooking skills. He was born in China and immigrated to America prior to 1880, arriving in the city within the next decade. In 1891, Lucy was a partner in the Kay & Lucy Restaurant inside the Steiner Hotel. (See chapter 21.) However, his partnership with Kay didn't last long, and Lucy left the city for a while.

He returned to North Yakima from California in 1894 and started a multigenerational Chinese restaurant. It would last approximately thirty-nine years and be owned by several Wong family members. It would also become one of the few Chinese-owned restaurants in Japan Town.

In August 1894, Lucy announced he was opening the Richelieu Restaurant in the storehouse of the Terry Stone Building. Prior to opening, he made several improvements to the building, including the installation of possibly the first broiler in the city. The Richelieu Restaurant opened on September 2, 1894.

The Terry Stone Building was located on the south side of East Yakima Avenue, at the southwest corner of the East Yakima Avenue and First Street intersection. In 1890, the three-story building served as a barrier

The Terry Stone Building *left*, where the Richelieu Restaurant opened in 1894.

that helped to prevent the spread of a tragic fire in the city. Four years after the fire, the Richelieu Restaurant opened its doors on the main floor of the Terry Stone Building.

Lucy operated the Richelieu Restaurant successfully enough over the next few years that, by the end of 1897, he had purchased the City Restaurant as well. He operated the Richelieu Restaurant as the finer dining facility, while the City Restaurant was operating twenty-four hours a day. Of the two restaurants, it was the Richelieu that withstood time. In 1898, Lucy was charging twenty-five and fifty-cents for his meals, which often included goose, turkey, fish, game, oysters and other in-season delicacies. Parties and social gatherings were often held at his restaurant.

The following year, the building itself underwent changes. In 1901, it was sold to Dr. George Sloan of Roslyn. Dr. Sloan and his brother Alexander D. Stone proceeded to make significant changes to the structure, including reducing it from three stories to two. They completed the changes in 1902 at a cost of $14,000. The businesses on the first floor included the North Yakima Drug Store—run by the Sloan family, with Dr. Sloan's brother Alexander being the most noted—and the Richelieu Restaurant, with its entrance on East Yakima Avenue.

When the restaurant opened in the new building, it had dropped the Richelieu name. It was listed simply as a restaurant run by Hop Wong at

The Sloan Building, with the Richelieu Restaurant located on the right side, circa 1902–07.

22 East Yakima Avenue. Lucy appears to have still been involved in the restaurant, but it was primarily Hop who ran it successfully for years. In 1908, Hop and the restaurant became the center of two social and legal issues in the city.

In early 1908, Chief Short of the police department made a recommendation to the city council to remove all private boxes from restaurants and saloons that was followed with an ordinance passed by the city council. Hop Wong, along with Sam Chong, refused to comply and left their private boxes intact, hiring Henry Snively as their attorney. (See chapter 12.) However, private boxes weren't the only issue Hop faced in 1908.

In the summer of 1908, anti-Asian sentiment was on the rise, and rumors spread in papers throughout the Northwest of Chinese and Japanese restaurant owners taking over all the restaurant establishments in the city. Hop and his restaurant survived the social issues and continued to operate.

Two years later, Mr. Lucy Wong was running the restaurant, although Hop Wong was still working at the location as a cook. Sadly, Hop once again found himself in the middle of a social controversy when he and two other Chinese restaurant workers, Lee Fon and L.K. Dong, registered to vote in elections with the city clerk. Although all three men were Chinese, they were reported to be the first Japanese to register to vote in the city. Local politicians and others in the city had issues with the three registering, but the city clerk had allowed them to register since there was no law against it.

In 1914, Fong Wong took over the restaurant and renamed it the Richelieu. He ran the restaurant for approximately six years, until 1920, when he relocated to Ellensburg, Washington. Once in Ellensburg, he worked as a cook and lived in the hotel above the New York Café. (See chapter 14.)

The next owner, Sam Wong, also operated the café for only a few years before he moved to Ellensburg to work at the New York Café. But before leaving the city, he changed the café's name to the New Richmond Café. After Sam's departure, the restaurant had one final Wong family owner before its permanent closure.

You Guay Wong was born in Canton, China, in January 1881. It is unknown when he came to America, but he made several trips back to China. It was there that he married Dong Shee Wong. Their oldest son was born in China in 1917 before the family was able to come to the country.

In the mid-1920s, the You and Dong Shee Wong family were living in Yakima on South First Street, just south of the Tieton Hotel. You was in his forties when he took over the New Richmond Café; in 1928, they were still running the restaurant. Meanwhile, the family had expanded to include four sons, three of which were born in Yakima. Although living in a separate building, the restaurant was a family affair, and the boys were known to help wash dishes.

You and his family ran the New Richmond Café for approximately five more years before disaster struck. In December 1933, the city experienced a horrendous flood. Water covered entire streets, damaging and destroying several buildings in the city. The New Richmond Café was damaged from the flood, and the business closed permanently. Sadly, the building that the Wongs lived in was also devastated. The family was without a home or a business. It was the end of a thirty-nine-year family-owned restaurant that had started in China Town and continued to operate successfully in Japan Town.

After the loss of the restaurant and their residence, the You Wong family moved into a shack on South First Street near Union Gap, Washington. To help support themselves, they raised vegetables on the property and brought them to Yakima, where they sold them to grocers and other businesses. Another son and daughter joined the family while living at their new location.

You Wong died in Yakima in January 1959, twenty-two years after the loss of the restaurant. Dong Shee Wong passed away in April 1967. Four of their five boys returned to Yakima after either joining the military or receiving a higher education. They went on to build hydroplanes and set a record at Green Lake, Washington, with a boat they built. Their youngest son became an engineer and worked as a consultant on NASA's lunar Apollo missions. Another worked for the Golden Wheel Restaurant before retiring. The Wongs' daughter married and moved to Seattle as an adult.

After the flood, the Sloan Building remained standing. Repairs were made and, over time, various businesses operated from within the building. The Sloan Building was eventually torn down. Today, a parking lot and drive-through bank stand at its location.

14

THE GOLDEN WHEEL RESTAURANT

From 1905 to 1910, the Treat-Raynor Hardware Company was located at 15 South First Street. The company was jointly owned by Emerson Treat and Sinese C. Raynor. The two had purchased the company from David R. Barton of the Barton Hardware Company in 1904. Six years after purchasing the company, Emerson and Sinese moved their business to 11 South First Street, two doors north of the original location.

Although some modifications to the building may have occurred to accommodate the hardware store at 11 South First Street, little is known about the building itself. The Treat-Raynor Company conducted business at the location until 1919, when Emerson became the sole proprietor and the company was renamed the Treat Hardware Company. Goods sold at the store were typical of the day, ranging from hardware and seeds to kitchen stoves and cutlery.

Emerson's son Gaylord was working at the store as a bookkeeper in 1931, then he became the store manager. By 1934, he was his father's business partner. Father and son ran the company at the location until late 1936 or early 1937, when they relocated to the opposite side of South First Street, leaving the location vacant. The next business to occupy the building was also owned by a partnership that evolved into a multigenerational family-owned business.

In the 1930s, six partners of the New York Café in Ellensburg, Washington, decided to expand their restaurant business to Yakima. The partners were On Chin, Ng Mon Wai, Eddie Huie, Won Wai, Wong Jaw and Oywah

The original partners of the New York Café in Ellensburg, Washington. *From left*: Ng Mon Wai, On Chin, Won Wai, Oywah "Walter" Chin, Wong Jaw and Eddie Huie. *Leon Mon Wai.*

(Walter) Chin. In 1937, two of the partners, On Chin and Ng Mon Wai, relocated to Yakima and opened the Golden Wheel Restaurant at Treat Hardware Company's former location. The location was well within the parameters of the once thriving—but now less prominent—China Town district of the city.

On Chin was born in Seattle, Washington, in April 1888 to Gong Cok Han Chin and Yan Hong of Taishan, Guangdong, China. (Taishan is considered the first home of the overseas Chinese.) His parents arrived in the Pacific Northwest to work for the railroad during a tumultuous time for Chinese immigrants. (See China Town.) His family is reported to have moved back to China when On was a child as a result of anti-Chinese sentiment. However, it wasn't long before On returned.

In 1907, On returned to the United States to find work and help support his family in China. After two years, he was able to save enough money to return home to visit. At the age of twenty-three, he had returned to America and was living in Ellensburg. It was there that he found work as a dishwasher and waiter at the New York Café. It had been established in 1911 by Huie Doo Toang and Won Wai, also immigrants from Taishan.

On continued to work at the New York Café, making occasional trips back to China. On one trip in March 1917, he married his first wife, Louie Hong Shee. Afterward, he returned to Ellensburg. Although his wife was never able to immigrate to America, he often returned to China for visits, and the couple had five children, some of whom would return to Ellensburg with On at a young age.

In 1920, On was still residing in Ellensburg, working at the New York Café and living in the hotel located above it. Others living in the hotel with him were Chinese immigrants who also had past or future ties to Yakima. Fong Wong had previously lived in Yakima, running the Richelieu. (See chapter 13.) Mr. N. Mon Wai was the son of Won Wai and a future business partner of On in Yakima.

While On was working in Ellensburg, his first wife, Louie Hong Shee, who was still living in China, became ill and died. On and his children who had moved to America with him returned to China for her burial. Later, in 1932, On returned to China and married his second wife, Wong Yok Lon Chin. Like his first wife, she would remain in China while On returned to Ellensburg.

Members of the On Chin family in 1937, the same year the Golden Wheel opened in Yakima. *Front row*: Frank Chin, Wong Yoke Lon Chin, James Chin (in Wong Yoke Lon's lap), Wayne Chin, On Chin, Sue Chin Lee (in On's lap), Joe Chin and Moy Chin. *Back row*: Jade Chin, Calvin Chin, Ten Gim Chin and Louie Chin. *Maylee Chin Witham.*

On eventually become a partner in the New York Café with Eddie Huie (son of the original founder) and Ng Won Wai. The three operated the New York Café in Ellensburg until 1937, when On and Mon Wai (son of Won Wai) relocated to Yakima to open the Golden Wheel Restaurant. Eddie Huie, Won Wai and Oywah (Walter) Chin stayed in Ellensburg to run the café there.

Ng Mon Wai, On's partner at the Golden Wheel Restaurant, was born in Har-Pin, Kwangtung, China. He was the son of Won Wai and had traveled from China to Seattle at the age of twelve to join his father in Ellensburg. A decade later, at twenty-three years of age, he was working at the café with his father and living in the hotel above it.

While living in both Ellensburg and Yakima, Mon Wai also made several trips back to China to see family. In February 1940, while in China, he married his second wife, Faye Mon Wai. Mon Wai returned to Yakima shortly afterward. His second wife was able to join him in Yakima the following spring. Once in Yakima, the couple raised their children while Mon Wai helped run the Golden Wheel.

On's second wife, Wong Yok Lon, was able to join her husband in Yakima in the early 1940s as well. Their three children, as well as several of On's children from his first marriage, were now located in Yakima, where they were raised alongside Mon Wai's children.

Although the Golden Wheel Restaurant was successful, social issues did affect the families in the early 1940s. When World War II began, like elsewhere, some confusion regarding the distinction between the Chinese and Japanese occurred. As a result, On felt compelled to wear a button indicating he was Chinese. Unfortunately, some in the city could not tell the difference.

In addition, the restaurant was located directly across the street from Yakima's thriving Japan Town. With the evacuation of the Japanese from the city, their families lost friends and business acquaintances. Regardless, On Chin and Mon Wai's families and their restaurant endured, including one of On's creations.

In the 1930s, while at the New York Café, On created the New York Salad Dressing. It became popular among patrons of the café as well as those outside of Ellensburg. When On moved to Yakima to open the Golden Wheel Restaurant, the dressing continued to gain popularity. Several family members who worked at the restaurant recall having to make, bottle, label and, of course, serve the dressing at the restaurant. The dressing was sold at various locations into the 1940s and is still served at the Golden Wheel.

Right: Ng Mon Wai, one of the original co-owners of the Golden Wheel Restaurant. *Justin Momeai*.

Below: Grand opening of the Golden Wheel Restaurant, 1937. In the back row are the three original owners (*left to right*): On Chin, Ng Mon Wai and Eddie Huie, who stayed in Ellensburg to run the New York Café. *Justin Momeai*.

On Chin started as a young dishwasher at the New York Cafe in Ellensburg and eventually became the owner of several restaurants. The Golden Wheel was his last restaurant before he retired in 1965. He believed education was the key to success and encouraged all of his children's educational pursuits. As a result, his descendants have achieved college bachelor's, master's and PhD degrees in many occupations and professions. Some have become restaurant owners in Washington (such as the Golden Kayland and Jade Tree in Yakima and the Golden Pheasant in Sunnyside). Others became public administrators, government employees, architects, engineers, doctors, pharmacists, bankers, military officers and even a U.S. ambassador. On Chin passed away in July 1975, leaving behind a legacy of successful restaurant ownership as well as successful descendants.

Mon Wai eventually relocated to western Washington after retiring from the Golden Wheel Restaurant in 1975. He passed away in Bellevue, Washington, in July 1990.

Throughout the history of the Golden Wheel, various changes were made to both the restaurant and the building. One of those changes included members of the family opening the Yakiman bar in the connecting building to the south of the restaurant. Perhaps the biggest change to the restaurant occurred in October 1982, when the structure caught fire. The entire building was redone, except for a wall that was left in place to maintain the historic value of the building. The exterior and interior of the building were completely revamped as a result. The adjacent bar operated by family members was moved to the back of the building that had once served as the restaurant's banquet area. The structural changes made after the fire remain today.

During the past eighty years, the restaurant has not only served its food to patrons, but it has also been a source of work for family members and acquaintances. Several family friends and past China Town business owners have worked at the restaurant over time. One of the Wong boys, whose parents owned the New Richmond Café in the early 1930s, worked for a time at the restaurant. (See chapter 13.) Sam Chong's son also worked at the restaurant after returning to Yakima and running his father's cigar store. (See chapter 12.)

The Golden Wheel Restaurant remains open today. It is the longest-running family-owned and operated restaurant in the city's history. It is also the longest-running Chinese-owned business in the city. The Golden Wheel is currently owned by the grandson of one of the original owners of the New York Café.

15

THE TIETON HOTEL AND DRAGON INN RESTAURANT

T win boys Judd and Grant Elliott were born in Illinois in 1869 to Joseph Elliott and his wife, Henrietta. The family moved west, arriving in North Yakima in 1901, where their father purchased a large piece of land and began fruit ranching. (The area would later become known as Elliott Heights.) Although the parents remained in Yakima, the boys lived in Seattle and became involved in successful business ventures. They would often return to North Yakima to see family, as well as to erect a building that remains standing today.

In the spring of 1908, Judd and Grant, also known as the Elliott Brothers, spent $38,000 to have a building erected on the southeast corner of South First Street and East Chestnut. Once completed, the upper two floors of the building served as the Tieton Hotel, with William B. Ross as the proprietor. William's time as the proprietor was not lengthy, nor was the ownership of the building by the Elliott Brothers. In February 1910, the Elliott Brothers sold the building to the Iler Investment Company for $73,000. The sale earned the brothers almost twice what they had spent building it.

Various proprietors of the Tieton Hotel occupied the building for more than a decade. It took until 1922 for the hotel to finally have a proprietor who would remain at the location for more than a couple of years. M.P. Baldwin took over the Tieton Hotel and served as the proprietor for the next thirteen years. In 1930, the hotel had twenty rooms, and Baldwin charged one dollar and up per day to stay in some of the best beds in the city. He would run the hotel for five years.

The Tieton Hotel, on the southeast corner of South First Street and East Chestnut.

The Tieton Hotel, on the southeast corner of South First Street and East Chestnut, July 1909.

In 1935, Mary Chadwick became the proprietor of the hotel. She ran the business until 1942, when it again experienced an influx of proprietors. It took another decade before the Tieton Hotel was purchased by a family that would operate the hotel and, later, a restaurant on the main floor.

Franklin Lyen was born in New York on August 5, 1921. His wife, Sun Choi Wan, was born in China in 1919. The couple married in China on April 7, 1953. It was Sun's second marriage. Within a year of their marriage, the couple was living in Yakima and had become the proprietors of the Tieton Hotel. More than a decade later, one of Sun's sons arrived in the city and became part of the family's business in the building.

Benny Kwong was born in China in November 1938. He arrived in the country around the age of eleven and lived in New York for a number of years before arriving in Yakima prior to 1960. From approximately 1960 to 1963, Benny was a partner at the Skyline Restaurant (on Washington Avenue) with Paul Mon Wai and Yue Eng. Then, in 1964, Benny opened the Dragon Inn Restaurant on the main floor of his parents' hotel. With the opening of his restaurant, Benny and his parents would ensure the continuance of family business in the building for another three decades.

The year 1965 was a big one for the family. Benny was not only running the Dragon Inn Restaurant; he also took over proprietorship of the Tieton Hotel from his parents. Franklin and Sun retired and moved to King County, Washington. However, business wasn't the only thing changing for Benny that year.

In August 1965, Benny traveled to Whatcom County and married Sui (Susie) Wan Jai. Susie was born, and was still living, in Vancouver, British Columbia, at the time of their marriage. Afterward, the couple returned to Yakima, where Bennie continued to manage the restaurant and the hotel.

The mid-1970s brought change to the building. After more than seventy years of the building housing the Tieton Hotel, Bennie finally closed the hotel on the upper two floors. He began renting the rooms as apartments instead. Various people resided in the building, including other Chinese families, until at least the later part of the 1980s

Although the upper two floors of the building no longer served as a hotel, Bennie continued to operate the Dragon Inn Restaurant from the main floor. In 1994, he closed his restaurant and retired. In December of that year, Bennie and Susie moved to Newcastle, Washington. Thirteen years later, on June 25, 1997, Bennie Kwong passed away. His mother, his wife, a son and two brothers survived him.

After the closing of the Dragon Inn Restaurant, another restaurant, the Be'Same Mucho Mexican Grill, opened in the building. It lasted only a few years. The building has stood empty for several years, and the upper floors have served as various forms of storage.

Today, the building has a different owner who is rejuvenating the historic Tieton Hotel into apartments or condominiums on the upper floors and retail on the main floor.

16

THE GEE LUNG COMPANY
AND THE SUN YEE LUNG COMPANY

Sim Chin was born in China and immigrated to the United States in 1881. By 1900, he was in North Yakima and the co-owner of the Gee Lung Company. Located at 130 South First Street, the company stood just north of the South First Street and East Chestnut intersection, on the west side of North First Street.

Sim's partner in the company at the time was Charlie Rounds. The two men sold various Oriental goods and groceries like dry goods, rice, teas, imported Chinese and Japanese silks and wares.

Little is known about Charlie, but the partnership with Sim did not last long. By February 1902, Charlie had sold his interest in the company to Sim, who continued to sell the same type of goods, although he also added contracting for labor to the company.

Change in business wasn't the only big event to happen in 1902 for Sim. The same year, his son Chan Chin, who had been born in China the year before Sim left for America, arrived in the city to join his father. Chan was approximately twenty-two years old when he arrived in the city and became a partner in his father's business.

By 1903, Sim Chin had other partners in the Gee Lung Company. They were his son Chan, Soon Chin, Nung Ah and Tung Ah. With anti-Chinese sentiment still strong in the country, it was a rough time for the business partners. Nung Ah was trying to get his son Hop Ah to join him in the city, much as Sim Chin had. Chinese wishing to enter the country had to prove they were not laborers, an issue that was problematic for the Ahs.

Nung Ah's petition to allow his sons entry into the country resulted in agents of the Department of Commerce Immigration Service arriving in the city from Port Townsend, Washington. They visited the city to investigate Nung Ah as well as the Gee Lung Company. After interviewing Sim Chin, investigating the Gee Lung Company and interviewing Nung Ah, it was decided that Nung Ah was not a laborer, nor was Hop Ah. The investigation also revealed that the Gee Lung Company was a legitimate mercantile firm with substantial stock. The Department of Commerce Immigration Service recommended that the petition for Hop Ah's entry be granted.

The following year, in 1904, Chan Chin was still a partner in his father's business. However, he also opened his own business just north of his father's, at 128 South First Street. Chan's business, the Sun Yee Lung Company, sold Chinese groceries and silks. Father and son successfully ran their two stores next to one another. They became well liked in the city and were reported as being wealthy. Sadly, their wealth would also become part of Chan's future marriage issues.

In January 1908, at the age of twenty-eight, Chan returned to China to find a bride. He had also hoped to bring his mother to the city. However, he returned to North Yakima by the summer of 1908 unmarried and without his mother.

At some point, Chan had converted to Christianity and was attending the First Baptist Church. It was there that he met and fell in love with a sixteen-year-old white girl named Tina James. The two courted for a time, and Chan asked her father for permission to marry Tina. Her father objected to the marriage when Chan refused to pay him $300 for Tina, like traditional Chinese. Chan refused to pay Tina's father because he had become a Christian and was not following Chinese traditions. The two men disagreed over the payment for Tina, as did Sim and Tina's fathers.

Tina's mother on the other hand wasn't convinced that payment for her daughter was necessary. She gave the two permission to marry and witnessed their wedding on August 14, 1908, by Reverend Frank Whitney at the First Baptist Church.

Chan and Tina immediately traveled to the lower valley after the ceremony for their honeymoon, as well to escape Tina's father. They did return to the city, and Chan finally payed Tina's father a reported $500 for Tina, with an additional $6 for his new mother-in-law. Once the dispute was over, Chan and Tina moved into the building that his father, Sim, lived in. It was the same building that housed the Gee Lung Company and the Sun Yee Lung Company.

In 1909, the year after their marriage, Chan opened a restaurant within the building that the family had stores in. It lasted only a year. The following year, the family was still living at the location as well as running both stores and a boardinghouse there.

The Chins continued to run their stores successfully for several years. In 1920, they are noted as moving to Los Angeles. While there, Chan and Tina added more children to their family, for a total of three boys and six girls. A year and a half after their last son was born, Chan, 45, passed away on December 27, 1925. Tina eventually moved to Tucson, Arizona, and died at the age of 101 on May 24, 1994.

Their store closed when they moved, ending a successful era of business in Yakima. No information is known about the buildings that once housed the Gee Lung Company and Sun Yee Lung Company. Presently, a brick building stands at the site, but it is unknown if it is the building that had housed the two companies.

PART IV

JAPAN TOWN

The 1890s saw the immigration of several Japanese to the valley. Of those arriving, most were engaged in farming in the lower valley. However, not all who came to the area were inclined to do agricultural work. Some worked as laborers for the railroad when the companies refused to continue to hire Chinese.

By the early 1900s, many Japanese immigrants who worked in other industries began arriving in the city. They included merchants, hotel owners, cooks and restaurant owners, as well as their employees and families. Most, but not all, of the early Japanese business owners coming to the city opened their businesses on a block located within China Town (between South Front Street, East Yakima Avenue, South First Street and East Chestnut).

With the opening of the Japanese businesses on the block came the increase of their employees as well as their families. Soon, the block became a thriving area known as Japan Town by locals. Japan Town was not necessarily visually evident, due to a lack of Asian decor on the buildings. Whites owned the buildings, and the Japanese businessmen leased from them. By the 1920s, Japan Town had begun to flourish; by 1940, it dominated the block.

Life for the early Japanese Americans living and working in the city was not easy. They experienced several social and racially related issues. Some of their restaurants were the center of accusations, and they were often encouraged to stay within their district. Regardless, the Japanese community in Yakima generously contributed to the city and its citizens.

One such contribution occurred in 1909, when North Yakima's Fourth of July celebrations were canceled for lack of funding. The Japanese in the city donated 150 fireworks worth $200 so that the citizens could celebrate the holiday. The following year, they contributed two six-inch guns, thought to be the biggest in the Pacific Northwest, as well as two three-inch guns, for shooting off fireworks for the celebration. Such actions earned the Japanese living in the city the respect of many citizens.

By the 1920s, racism was gaining momentum in the valley and the city. Decisions refusing to grant citizenship to Japanese immigrants were being upheld in the U.S. Supreme Court, resulting in some Japanese immigrants being unable to become citizens. Meanwhile, it was illegal for Japanese immigrants to own property. Immigration status and property ownership weren't the only issues at the time.

In the spring of 1923, large Ku Klux Klan gatherings occurred in Yakima County, one of which was less than two blocks east of Japan Town. An estimated two thousand Klan followers gathered at Yakima's Capitol Theater to hear Reverend C. Curtis of Vancouver, Washington, speak. In August 1924, another large gathering occurred in a field outside of the city. Meanwhile, in the 1920s and '30s, some members of local organizations such as the American Legion and some Granges began to show disdain for the Japanese in both the city and the valley.

Things took a horrific turn for those of Japanese heritage with the bombing of Pearl Harbor and the onset of America's involvement in World War II. Anger toward those of Japanese heritage rose quickly in the country. Some influential Americans struggling to compete with Japanese in businesses and farming took advantage of the situation and applied pressure to politicians, lobbyists and Congress. As a result of the nationwide anti-Japanese sentiment, President Franklin Roosevelt signed into law Executive Order No. 9066 on February 19, 1942.

Not everyone in government was in favor of the internment of the Japanese. When the issue was heard in hearings, the Department of Justice opposed the executive order for its concept and its ethical impact on the country. Regardless, the government moved forward with Executive Order No. 9066 and used the U.S. Army to assist with the evacuation from the West Coast of all persons of Japanese heritage deemed a threat to national security.

The effects of the anti-Japanese sentiment and the executive order was felt heavily in Yakima Valley. Those of Japanese heritage in the area were not initially included in the order and were outside the areas specifically noted. However, local members of the Klan, as well as some members of the local American Legion and Granges, wanted anyone of Japanese heritage gone from the city and the valley. To ensure their evacuation, they met with local and state representatives and were able to convince them to extend the original designated evacuation areas to Yakima County.

Not everyone wanted the Japanese out of the area. Several prominent people in the area spoke against the removal of the Japanese, defending their right to be in the valley and trying to convince authorities and politicians otherwise. One such person was the existing City of Yakima attorney, who worked with other attorneys in the state to prevent the extension of the evacuation area to Yakima. However, their attempts to block the expansion were unsuccessful.

With the addition of Yakima to Executive Order No. 9066, those of Japanese heritage in the city were forced to pack their personal and business properties and leave the city. While some were lucky enough to have people who could watch and care for the items, many were forced to sell almost everything they owned, often receiving far less than the items' worth.

With the departure of the Japanese from the city, Yakima lost a large group of hardworking, law-abiding citizens who contributed not only to the vibrancy of the city but also to the society, economy and overall success of the city. With their departure, Yakima's Japan Town vanished. After the closure of the internment camps, none of those owning businesses within the city returned to reopen business.

THE SUNSET CAFÉ

One of the buildings moved from Old Town Yakima to North Yakima was that of the Lillie House. Originally the home to the Charles B. Lillie family, it also served as a hotel.

Born in Massachusetts on August 5, 1819, Charles Lillie enlisted in the military on February 22, 1862. He served in Company B, Nineteenth Wisconsin Infantry, for three years before being discharged in April 1865. Fourteen years later, Charles was living in Old Town with his family and working as a carpenter.

When North Yakima was established by the railroad and the offer to move businesses and homes to the new city occurred, the Lillie family moved their house and business to the new city. They placed their home on the northeast corner of South Front Street and East Chestnut, where it would continue to operate as a hotel. It would eventually become known as the Old Lillie House.

In 1891, Charles was admitted to the Washington Soldiers Home in Orting, Washington, for his declining health. He would reside there until he died of Bright's disease in January 1897. During his absence and after his death, the care and operation of the Old Lillie House was left to children, with his son Nevada Lillie handling many of the decisions regarding the building. However, his involvement in the property was often overshadowed by other activities he was involved in.

Nevada "Vade" Lillie was well known for his various roles in the valley. While he lived in Old Town, he drove a stagecoach for his brother between

Old Town and Goldendale. He was married to Josephine Bowser when she became the founder of Toppenish. Later in life, he served as a deputy sherriff. During most of this time, the family had other businesses located within their building.

In the early 1890s, a restaurant called the Yakima Kitchen opened in the Old Lillie House. In 1894, the Yakima Kitchen failed when its new owner left town on the train to avoid paying debts. The space was then occupied by other businesses, including a fruit stand and a bakery.

Nevada H. Lillie, son of Charles Lillie, 1883. *Mr. William Brown.*

In 1895, Nevada announced that he was considering modifying the Old Lillie House and placing a block structure on the site. However, it wasn't until December 1899, when several of the other old hotels were undergoing modifications, that Nevada was reported as having improvements made to it.

A decade later, in 1905, the location would become the controversial site of a saloon owned by Theodore Steiner. Theodore was a well-respected businessman who owned several buildings in North Yakima and Kittitas Counties. He applied for a permit to open a saloon in the building at a time when saloons were not well received in the city. After much debate with the city council and help from his attorney, Fred Parker, Theodore was finally granted a permit. The saloon lasted only about five years before Theodore left North Yakima and moved to Kittitas County. His departure left a space in the building that would be filled by one of the city's early Japanese restaurant owners. It would continue to be the site of Japanese-owned restaurants for more than thirty-five years.

The first Japanese-owned restaurant to occupy 23 South Front Street was that of Kiyoshi Morikawa. Kiyoshi was born in Japan to a family with considerable wealth, allowing him to receive a good education. Afterward, he became a commissioned officer in the Japanese military and served in the Russo-Japanese War. He married his wife, Kazue, while in Japan; the couple had two young daughters.

According to a descendant, Kiyoshi immigrated to the United States as an adventurer, leaving his wife, children and parents in Japan. By 1910, Kiyoshi had arrived in North Yakima and had opened a lunch counter on

North Front Street. Not only was he a business owner at the time, but he also become a prominent member of the Japanese Association of Yakima County and was an active participant in the publishing of articles and magazines in the Japanese language. Toward the end of 1910, Kiyoshi was escorted to the train station by several people for the start of his return trip to Japan to visit family and bring his wife back to North Yakima. He returned within a year with Kazue, but his daughters Shigeko and Noriko stayed in Japan with his parents.

Once in the city, the couple didn't waste time reestablishing themselves as restaurant owners. By 1911, Kiyoshi and his wife had opened a restaurant on South Front Street in Nevada Lillie's building. The location also served as their residence, where they continued to expand their family, having five more children. Sadly, their son George Washington Morikawa, who was born on December 17, 1911, passed away on August 2, 1913. He was buried in Tahoma Cemetery, where the family would continue to bury their loved ones for generations to come. After George's death, the family continued to run their restaurant until 1914.

By 1915, the family had moved from the building and around the corner of East Chestnut to the U.S. Hotel. They lived in the hotel, where Kiyoshi worked, until 1917, when they once again moved back to the Lillie House. This time, they were one door south of where their restaurant had been located a few years earlier. It was there that they opened a Japanese store. It sold items ranging from candy to fresh vegetables and Japanese goods. In 1919, the family closed their store. It was the last business they owned in Yakima's Japan Town. However, it was not the end of the family's role in the valley's history.

Around 1920, Kiyoshi and Kazue's oldest daughter, Shigeko, who had remained in Japan, joined her husband, Shukichi Inaba, on his family's farm in the Lower Valley. When the Japanese were evacuated from the valley, she and other family members were moved to the Heart Mountain Wyoming Internment Camp. Afterward, they were one of the few families to return to the valley, where they continued farming. Shigeko, Shukichi, their children and, eventually, grandchildren, remained in the Lower Valley. Her descendants still own and operate Inaba Farms in Wapato, Washington.

After the Morikawas left their restaurant on South Front Street, a number of other Japanese business owners operated a restaurant from the location. Sam Nakamura ran a restaurant at the location from 1915 until 1922. He was followed by Akizo Mori, who ran it for approximately one year. It wasn't until 1923, when Mr. T. Tomito took over the restaurant, that it was named the Sunset Café. Tomito operated the Sunset Café for three years before the longest continual owner took over.

Bunjiro Tsutsui was born in Japan on October 5, 1877. By 1918, he had immigrated to the United States and was living in Yakima on North Front Street with his twenty-three-year-old wife, Kae, also from Japan. At the time, he was noted on his World War I Draft Registration Card as working as a laborer in Yakima. Sadly, within a month of completing his draft registration, Kae passed away in December 1918. Within two years of Kae's death, Bunjiro was operating a restaurant on South Second Street. He remarried a few years later and with his second wife, Tono, operated the O.W. Market and Café in the city. They ran the market and restaurant for a few years and in 1926 became the next owners of the Sunset Café. After living elsewhere for a number of years—and three years after acquiring the restaurant—they also made it their home. Fourteen years later, in 1940, they would become the longest owners of the Sunset Café in the history of the city.

The last owner of the Sunset Café was Sam (Torakichi) Migita, who was no stranger to running a business. Sam was born in Japan about 1878 and immigrated to the country at the age of twenty-one. He came by boat from Alaska to Seattle in 1899, paying for his trip by working as a cabin boy. By 1902, he was in North Yakima working various jobs, including that of a gardener, laborer and truck driver. He also became active in the Japanese community, as well as the Yakima Buddhist Church in Wapato.

By 1918, Sam was married to his first wife, Tora, and operating a restaurant on East Chestnut. The couple was living with their baby daughter, Hisako, on East Walnut at the time. The family also had farming property in the Riverside area of Yakima. Although busy, the Migitas stayed in touch with their family in Japan. In 1918, Sam and Tora returned to Japan to visit. Hisako was approximately one when they returned from Japan to Seattle on the ship *Katori Maru*.

Sam eventually became the proprietor of the California Hotel on South Front Street. The family moved to the hotel as well. Tragically, it was while living at the hotel that Sam's family life would change. In December 1930, Hisako, then thirteen, contracted tuberculosis from one of the boarders. She died on December 13, 1930, as a result and was buried in Tahoma Cemetery. Just eight years later, he would lose his wife on September 30, 1938.

A decade after losing his daughter and two years after losing his wife, Sam Migita began operating the Sunset Café, just two lots south of the California Hotel. The following year, in 1941, he married his second wife, Momoye (Tanaka). They ran the Sunset Café for approximately one year before the

Torakichi "Sam" and Momoye Migita (of Yakima), seated in apartment 15-5-A in Heart Mountain, Wyoming, on April 11, 1945. *The George and Frank C. Hirahara Photograph Collection of Heart Mountain, Wyoming 1943–1945. Manuscripts, Archives, and Special Collections, Washington State University Libraries, Pullman, Washington.*

relocation of the Japanese in Yakima. They were the last Japanese owners of the Sunset Café in the city's history; in fact, they were the last owners at all of the Sunset Café.

Unlike most of the Japanese in Yakima, Sam and Momoye were initially relocated to the Tule Lake Internment Camp in Northern California. Later, they were relocated to the Heart Mountain Internment Camp in Wyoming, where they stayed with others from Yakima until the closure of the internment camp. The family moved to St. Louis afterward and never returned to Yakima to live.

Although Sam and Momoye did not return to Yakima, Sam was responsible for spending his personal individual allotted postage money to ship the religious items belonging to the Yakima Buddhist Church in Wapato back to Wapato.

The building from which the Sunset Café operated remained after the Migita family's departure. Other businesses occupied the building over time, including other restaurants like the El Progresso Café in 1951. By 1960, the building was vacant and, not long afterward, torn down. Today, the site is an empty gravel lot surrounded by wire fencing.

18

THE MONTANA HOTEL

One of the early families to settle in the Yakima Valley was that of David and Marie Guilland. David was born in a French area of Switzerland named Berne, in 1825. His wife, Marie, was born in 1831 to an Austrian aristocratic family living in a French area of Switzerland. The two met and married in Switzerland after David served as a Swiss army officer. Marie relinquished all of her royal rights to her aristocratic family. Before the age of forty, the couple would immigrate to America.

David and Marie arrived in North Carolina. Then, not long after, they were part of a French immigrant wagon train traveling from the East Coast to Colorado. The family stayed in Colorado while David worked as a coal miner then relocated to Oregon, where they started cattle ranching. It was there that they heard of Yakima Valley and decided to relocate. They moved north with their five living children and cattle.

The Guilland family arrived in the valley in 1861 and was soon met with disaster. The winter of 1861–62 was one of the worst experienced in the valley. The family lost approximately $10,000 of cattle in the storm. As a result, the family sold their remaining cattle and sought employment elsewhere. Luckily, they were able to transition from cattle ranching to a business that would make their family prominent in the history of the valley.

In 1875, David and Marie began building a house in Yakima City. Over time, he continued to add to the home. Eventually, their place became a two-story building with two smaller one-story buildings attached. Once completed, the family was living in the home and running the Guilland House Hotel from it. In 1884, when the railroad offered free lots in North Yakima, the Guillands became one of the first business owners to agree to move to the new city.

The Guillands hired a mover, who began preparing the Guilland Hotel in January 1885. In February, it began its long journey to North Yakima, moving approximately a quarter of a mile a day. Due to hostilities between those leaving Yakima City and those staying, David placed guards at both the front and back of the building during the entire move. Meanwhile, Marie managed to do the necessary chores to keep the hotel running while it was moving.

On February 27, 1885, the Guilland House finally arrived in North Yakima. The three building sections were placed at the northwest corner of South First Street and East Chestnut on a stone foundation that was laid at a cost of $850. The building operated successfully for the next decade as the family's home and the Guilland House hotel. Room rates were competitive with other hotels in the city. In 1889, rooms ranged from $1.50 to $2.00 a day, with a special rate for regular boarders. By the spring of 1897, the family changed the name of the hotel from the Guilland House to the Guilland Hotel. It wasn't the only thing that changed. At the time, it was advertising as the headquarters for traveling stockmen and reduced its rates to $1.00 per day, or $4.00 per week.

On September 30, 1900, David Guilland died of cardiac-related issues. Not only did his death leave his wife a widow, but it also ended an era for one of the city's oldest hotels. The couple's children were grown at the time of his passing, leaving Marie alone at the hotel. She moved to Portland, Oregon, to be closer to two of her daughters. It was there on December 29, 1909, that Marie died.

Three months after David's death, the Guilland Hotel was operating under a new manager, Aaron Christian Bollenbach. Born in Minneapolis, Minnesota, in 1870, Bollenbach was a bachelor when he began managing the hotel in January 1901. Within three months of taking over, he had restructured the prices for those staying at the hotel: $0.25 a night, or $1.00 or more for an entire day. Weekly stays were increased to between $4.50 and $5.00. Meals could also be purchased for $0.25 each.

The following spring, Aaron married a woman named Kate. Kate was two years younger than Aaron when they married. Unlike the Guillands, the couple did not live in the hotel. Rather, they lived in a house on Cherry Street until tragedy struck. Kate died just eighteen months after arriving in the city. At about the same time as his wife's death, Aaron's involvement with the Guilland House also ended. By 1903, the hotel was under the management of another individual. Although it wouldn't be the last time Aaron worked on the lot, his departure would be the end of what was once called the Guilland Hotel.

Sydney Eugene Varian was born about 1876 in Mason County, West Virginia. He arrived in North Yakima by the early 1900s and was running the old Guilland Hotel prior to 1905. Although it was the same building, he renamed it the Varian Hotel. Unmarried when he acquired the hotel, within a year, Sydney married Florence Helen from Nashville, Tennessee.

Although divorced in approximately five years, Sydney continued running the hotel and opening other businesses within it. He opened his own saloon, appropriately called the Varian Saloon, as well as leased out space to a restaurant, which would become one of the city's first Japanese-owned restaurants in the city.

With its doors facing South First Street, the Royal Café opened for business within the Varian Hotel in 1906. Its first owners, Mr. and Mrs. Frank Iwanaga, quickly earned a reputation as owning one of the finer Japanese restaurants in the city.

Frank Iwanaga was born in Japan in 1872, arriving in the country in his early twenties in 1893. Ten years later, he brought his twenty-one-year-old wife, Tomaki, also born in Japan, to America. The details of the couple's marriage are unknown, but within three years of Tomaki arriving in the country, they were living in North Yakima and were proprietors of the city's first Royal Café.

The opening of the Royal Café was an elaborate affair well noted in the city. Not long afterward, the Iwanagas held another well-remembered affair: a banquet honoring the birth of their first child, a son named Nabhito. The celebration included approximately seventy people from the city's Japanese community, as well as those in the Lower Valley and Ellensburg. Food specially ordered from Japan was served, along with a few American foods. Although a joyous and grand occasion, Frank and Tomaki celebrated with their guests only in the morning. They opened up the Royal Café for regular business in the afternoon. The Iwanagas' success did not end with the celebration of the birth of their son. They would continue running the café until major changes to the building occurred.

By summer 1907, Sydney Varian would no longer own or operate the Varian Hotel. Within a year, he acquired the U.S. Hotel, one building west of the lot on East Chestnut. He also relocated his Varian Saloon one lot west. Although he vacated the lot, like Aaron Bollenbach before him, he would return to it in the future to conduct business.

About the same time, Patrick Mullins arrived in North Yakima. A former wealthy mayor of Butte, Montana, he was a well-known, politically active, self-made man with a positive reputation that preceded his presence in the city. Prior to his arrival in the city, many already knew Mullins for his widely publicized speech in Butte when President Franklin Roosevelt visited.

In 1907, Patrick purchased the lot on which the old Guilland Hotel and Varian Hotel stood. He and his wife, Nellie, complemented each other in their business ventures. Patrick was business smart; Nellie handled the books.

Once Patrick purchased the Varian Hotel lot in 1907, he began making plans to tear down the historic building and erect a four-story brick structure. His plans to remove the Guilland Hotel building were expedited in September 1907, when a fire started on the roof. The damage was extensive, and the remains of the structure had to be torn down as a result.

The fire tragically ended the era not only of the historic Guilland Hotel building but also of the Iwanagas' Royal Café. The Iwanaga family relocated to King County, where Frank began working as a section foreman for the railroad; his wife, Tomaki, worked in the boarding industry. Their first son was now approximately three, and they added another son, Tsuguto, by 1910.

With the removal of the historic Guilland Hotel building, Mullins began the construction of his brick four-story structure. It was completed in 1909 and opened as the new and modern Montana Hotel on the upper floors. Like others in the city, the Mullinses owned the building but leased it out to other businesses. Wanting to make his accommodations up to date, in 1911, he had the city extend sewer lines to serve his new buildings.

Once completed, he leased out the upper floors as the Montana Hotel. The proprietor was Loretta L. Smith. Little is known of Smith with the exception that, by the summer of 1911, she had begun trying to sell the hotel to move to western Washington. The hotel did not sell immediately; she was still running it in January 1912 and then closed until September 1912, when it reopened under the new management of Mr. & Mrs. C.V. Sterling. Their management of the hotel was also short lived.

By 1917, Sydney Varian had returned to the lot and was living in the Montana Hotel with his third wife, Agnes, while operating his own hotel one lot west. Within a year, he would do more than live in the Montana Hotel building. He entered into a partnership with H.E. Bacon, and the two changed the name from the Montana Hotel to the Elk Hotel. Agnes worked as a clerk for the hotel.

Patrick Mullins continued to own the building during this time until he passed away on December 19, 1916. After his death, his son George Mullins took over ownership of the building, renting out the space to the others.

Sydney's second attempt at running a hotel on the lot did not last long. Just four years later, in 1921, he was shot in the arm by his partner, Mr. Bacon. Sydney was arrested after the incident and charged with assault. He continued to run the Elk Hotel for another year before finally ending his business dealings on the lot.

The Elk Hotel operated for a few more years until 1926, when it would once again undergo changes. The first change was its reverting to the name Montana Hotel. The second was the return of Sydney's predecessor, Aaron Bollenbach, as the proprietor with his second wife, Maud. His second term as proprietor at the location lasted approximately one year. Prior to his departure, a second Japanese restaurant was leased from the main floor.

Twenty years after the closing of the first Royal Café, Harry Nakumura opened the second Royal Café in the building. When Aaron Bollenbach was done as the proprietor of the Montana Hotel, Harry Nakumura took over the hotel's proprietorship. Although he served as the proprietor of the Montana Hotel for only about three years, he continued to operate the Royal Café from the building until 1942, with the evacuation of the Japanese in the city.

Tokichi Hara took over proprietorship of the Montana Hotel after Harry Nakumura in 1930. Tokichi successfully ran the hotel for over a decade until, like Harry—who was still running the Royal Café—Japanese citizens in the city were evacuated.

After Harry Nakumura and Tokichi Hara left the city, the Montana Hotel continued to operate on the upper floors of the building; other businesses operated on the main floor. Thirty years after the evacuations, the legacy of the lot came to a sudden end.

In 1972, a fire started in a restaurant located in the building, damaging various businesses, including a drugstore, record store and barbershop. The damage to the building was so extensive that it was torn down. Today, the lot is a paved parking lot.

19

THE PACIFIC HOTEL

In February 1903, the partnership of Alfred Kellog and Ernest Ford was granted permission from the City of North Yakima to construct a two-story building on two lots located on the west side of midblock South First Street, between East Yakima Avenue and East Chestnut. They wasted no time beginning construction, and by the summer of 1903, their two-story building was complete and ready for occupancy. The main floor was occupied by businesses, one of which was run by Ford himself, while the second floor was soon leased to another new partnership in the city. The partnership of George A. Gano and Ingram B. Turnell eventually led the building to be known as the Pacific Hotel for the next 114 years.

George Gano was born in Ohio in 1864. He arrived in Yakima County in 1889 at the age of twenty-five. Upon arrival, he worked a series of odd jobs, including selling sewing machines, before purchasing some property in Moxee, Washington, where he became a rancher. He was not known to be a hotel proprietor. However, in the summer of 1903, he entered into a hotel partnership with Ingram Turnell.

Turnell was approximately eleven years older than Gano. In 1853, he was born in Wisconsin, where he had worked as a railroad brakeman until he suffered a substantial injury to his hand. Afterward, he took on various other railroad jobs around the country and ended up working for the railroad in North Yakima. Once in the city, he also worked a job at a hotel. Eventually, he left his job at the Northern Pacific Railroad to become more involved in the hotel industry. It was this pursuit that lead to his partnership with George Gano.

In July 1903, the Gano and Turnell partnership rented the second floor of the newly constructed Kellog and Ford Building and opened the Pacific Hotel. Their agreement consisted of Gano purchasing the furniture and fixtures for the hotel and Turnell paying him back in August 1903. The partnership lasted only a short time.

After receiving no payment from Turnell, Gano filed an injunction. The case ended up in court, with Ingram Turnell buying out George Gano's part of the business and becoming the sole owner of the Pacific Hotel. He continued to run the hotel independently for about five more years. Under his care, the hotel began to flourish. It was host to several weddings and other events between 1903 and the summer of 1906 and was considered one of the finest hotels in town.

Being an independent hotel owner was evidently very profitable. So good, in fact, that Turnell didn't have enough rooms to continue to run the hotel in the building. As a result, it was announced that Ernest Ford would be adding a third floor to the building and Turnell's Pacific Hotel would occupy the second and third floors.

The addition of the third floor allowed the hotel to expand to an additional eleven rooms, with private baths and a bathroom in every other two new rooms. The third-floor addition proved to be successful, and people began calling the building the Pacific Hotel rather than the Kellog and Ford Building.

With an expanded hotel, several gatherings were held at the hotel, both small and large, including celebrations, conferences, club outings and more. Some of the events would turn out to be controversial in the community.

In May 1907, the first known all–colored men's baseball club was formed in a meeting held at the hotel. Since Ingram Turnell was considered at the time to be knowledgeable in the sport, he was elected as the team's manager at the meeting. The team was named the Black Socks. Very little information is known of the Black Socks after their formation.

In the fall of the same year, a conference was held at the hotel that would prove to be both ironic and prophetic. The conference, held by the Northwest Painters, Decorators and Paperhangers, was thought to be one of its most successful gatherings in the western part of the country. It included a variety of speakers, most focusing on employment in the trade.

Imagine the tone of the meeting when the opening address by group president Dan McDermott of Vancouver, B.C., was given. It was reported: "Concluding with…he commented on the recent race riots in Vancouver in which the Chinese and Japanese were still badly scared as the result of the recent turmoil. He hoped that both races would get out and feared that another riot would follow, as a shipload were expected to arrive either yesterday or today." The tone of the convention was parallel to the various racial, immigration and labor issues that North Yakima and the country were experiencing at that time. Within seventeen years, the tone of this convention would come full circle when the Pacific Hotel became one of the dominant buildings and major businesses in Yakima's Japan Town.

Not all gatherings at the Pacific Hotel were so controversial. In fact, several fun events were hosted at the hotel, including a large party celebrating the birthday of President Abraham Lincoln. The party was hosted by the Sons and Daughters of Illinois Organization in February 1908. Many of the city's citizens and businessmen attended the affair, which was reported as a success.

Business for Ingram Turnell and the Pacific Hotel seemed to be going well until October 1908, when it was reported that five judgements had been filed against both Turnell and his wife, Nellie, for monies owed. One of the judgements filed was from the building owner, Ernest Ford, who claimed he was owed $352 in rent. Turnell was reported as owing more than $11,000 in bills to various people. At the time of the judgements, the Yakima Trust Company assumed ownership of the hotel, keeping Ingram Turnell on staff as manager for a short time.

The hotel is not all Turnell lost. During his hotel issues, he was also running for the North Yakima Fifth Ward city councilman position. With the public announcement of his losing the hotel, he withdrew his name from the election. The man who had built a hotel from nothing, expanded it from one floor to two floors and then lost it all approximately five years later would eventually become a fruit grower. He died on April 27, 1925, in Yakima.

With Turnell's departure, others ran the Pacific Hotel; various businesses occupied the ground floor. However, it wasn't until 1925 that the hotel became managed by the George Hirahara family, who brought it back to the successful business it once was.

George Hirahara was born in Wakayama Prefecture in Japan in 1905 to Motokichi Hirahara and his wife, Sato Hirahara. In 1907, when George was just two years old, Motokichi left Japan for the United States and moved to Tacoma.

Due to the Gentlemen's Agreement of 1907, the United States agreed to accept Japanese immigrants already residing in the country. The agreement also allowed for the immigration of their wives and children from Japan. This was fortuitous for Motokichi Hirahara to establish his residency in 1907 and to be able to use this as his legal entrance to the United States. He went back to Japan in 1909, as written in his World War II War Relocation Authority documents, and came back with his wife, Sato, and son George in 1910 to establish their residency in Tacoma.

Later that year, they settled in the Lower Valley area of Yakima County and began farming alongside other Japanese immigrants. Ten years after arriving, they were successful enough to lease a 160-acre farm in the Lower Valley.

While helping his family on their farm, their son George attended Yakima County Grammar School from September 1911 to June 1919 and then attended Wapato High School for one year. In 1924, his father sent him back to Japan for a five-month visit. What he didn't tell his son was that he had privately arranged for George to marry an eighteen-year-old girl named Koto Inoue from a neighboring town in Japan, through a "picture bride" arrangement. For George to return to the United States, he had to get married. The couple wed and returned to the state of Washington in June 1924 to live with his parents. Koto would become one of the last Japanese "picture brides" to enter this country.

Once back in the Yakima Valley with Koto, George had no interest in farming. As a result, a year after returning, he took a job working at the Pacific Hotel, and the two moved into their own apartment on the second

George and Koto Hirahara with baby Frank Hirahara, taken at the Harsch Photo Studio by Howard A. Harsch in Yakima, 1926. *The Hirahara Family Collection, Anaheim Public Library, Anaheim, California.*

Left: Koto Hirahara, thirty-six, wearing a military motif outfit, on the back patio of the Pacific Hotel. It is one of the last photos the Hirahara family took before leaving Yakima in June 1942. *The Hirahara Family Collection, Yakima Valley Museum, Yakima, Washington.*

Right: The Hiraharas had a patio in the back of the building where people could meet and talk. Young Frank Hirahara is shown standing on the back patio during winter. *The Hirahara Family Collection, Yakima Valley Museum, Yakima, Washington.*

floor. It was located on the north side of the building, and they soon turned it into a comfortable living space.

The following year, in 1926, the Hiraharas had their only child, Frank Hirahara. After Frank's birth, the family continued to live in the hotel for seventeen years. While growing up in the hotel, Frank spent time playing the trumpet and violin, studying, helping at the hotel and, of course, enjoying the family's private rooftop deck in the back of the building.

The birth of Frank was not the only big thing to occur for the Hirahara family in 1926. A year after working at the Pacific Hotel, they decided to purchase the sixty-room hotel. George did not purchase the building itself, rather just the Pacific Hotel. At the time, it was legal for first-generation Japanese immigrants to own a business, but not a building or property.

During the seventeen years that the George Hirahara family ran the Pacific Hotel, it once again flourished. Business was prosperous for the family, earning $5,000 per year. A sign on the outside of the building advertised that, at one time, they had steam heat and hot and cold water. Their rooms cost fifty cents and up. The hotel appeared to be thriving, and well-known visitors to the city were often reported as staying there.

From 1925 to 1942, the Hirahara family continued to gain a reputation as successful hotel owners. Part of their success may have been due to George's ability to manage hotel affairs such as booking reservations, assigning rooms, establishing hotel policy and supervising workers. He was also handy in carpentry, plumbing, electricity, paper hanging, printing and decorating, allowing him to make many of the hotel's improvements.

When George Hirahara wasn't working, he enjoyed fishing, hunting, sumo, baseball and photography. The Hirahara family was also very involved socially with the American and Japanese community in the Lower Valley. They were members of the Yakima Buddhist Church, as well as being friends with those living in Yakima's Japan Town.

Son Frank C. Hirahara was also very active in school. He attended Barge Elementary School, Washington Junior High School and Yakima High School alongside the other children in the city. He was a member of his school's track team and marching band, playing trumpet. He began his love of photography at the age of twelve. (His common interests with his father would eventually help to preserve the history of not only the hotel but also that of the Japanese in the Yakima Valley.)

Life for the Hirahara family at the Pacific Hotel was prosperous until the start of World War II. With the increased social pressures applied by not only the government but also some of the citizens of Washington State and the Yakima Valley, their lives would sadly change. The Hiraharas were forced to pack their belongings and leave their home and hotel business behind.

Since George Hirahara had made many Caucasian friends in Yakima, Oscar A. Beard and Harold Adams—who ran their Yakima Seed Store on the first floor of the building—were willing to give personal references for the Hirahara family. George retained counsel from Yakima attorney Elery Van Diest. Real estate broker Charles A. Marsh handled the family's property and business affairs while they were away from the city.

Because of their contacts, they were able to pack and store most of their personal belongings and some of the hotel items they owned in other locations in Yakima prior to leaving for the Portland Assembly Center

Right: The Pacific Hotel entrance, with lodgers standing in front. The sign states that the hotel had steam heat, hot and cold water and rooms for rent at fifty cents and up, with special rates available by the week. *The Hirahara Family Collection, Yakima Valley Museum, Yakima, Washington.*

Below: The Pacific Hotel, located at 10½ South First Street. The hotel was managed by George and Koto Hirahara in 1925 and then purchased by the Hiraharas in 1926. *The Hirahara Family Collection, Yakima Valley Museum, Yakima, Washington.*

and then the Heart Mountain Japanese American Incarceration Camp in Wyoming. Such items would later become part of the city's history at the Yakima Valley Museum and part of the Hirahara Family Collections at Washington State University, and the City of Anaheim, California. In addition, two items were donated to the Japanese American Collection at the Smithsonian National Museum of American History in Washington, D.C.

George and Frank C. Hirahara would go on to take and create the largest private collection of photographs taken by two amateur photographers at the Heart Mountain, Wyoming Japanese American Incarceration Camp, from 1943 to 1945. The more than two thousand original black-and-white negative photographic collection was created in a secret underground darkroom below the Hirahara family apartment. The darkroom needed to be kept a secret, since George was an alien and not allowed to possess a camera and take photographs in the camp. The collection has been donated to Frank C. Hirahara's alma mater, Washington State University in Pullman, Washington.

Prior to the closing of Heart Mountain, George inquired about the acceptance of his family returning to Yakima. In a May 23, 1945 letter from the U.S. Department of the Interior, Yakima Office, relocation officer Murray E. Stebbins wrote, "Charles Marsh spoke very highly of Mr. Hirahara and is anxious to cooperate with him in every way that he possibly can to assist George Hirahara to re-establish himself in Yakima." In another letter, dated June 15, 1945, from the U.S. Department of the Interior, War Relocation Authority, Stebbins wrote, "Mr. Hirahara enjoys a very fine reputation in Yakima and I am very anxious to be of assistance to him in every possible manner."

With assurances that he was welcomed back to Yakima, George Hirahara and his family left Heart Mountain, Wyoming, on October 2, 1945, driving his own car back to Yakima. Because his family no longer owned the Pacific Hotel, they drove to a home his family owned prior to the war at 21 East Washington Avenue and First Street. They became one of the first families to return to Yakima of the only 10 percent of Japanese American families who returned to the Yakima Valley.

Through the hard work and dedication of Frank's daughter Patti Hirahara, of Anaheim, California, the preservation and education of the history of the Japanese families who lived in the Yakima Valley are now being told. Her donation of the Hirahara family's artifacts, documents and photographs, and the Hirahara Family Collections, have helped educate people throughout the country. They are on display in many museums. Patti feels that the Yakima Valley is a second home for her, since her great-grandparents Motokichi and Sato Hirahara and grandparents George and Koto Hirahara are buried in Yakima's Tahoma Cemetery.

The Pacific Hotel's historic role in the city, as well as its role in Yakima's Japan Town, were lost with the relocation of the Yakima Valley Japanese community. Not long after the Hiraharas departure, the upper two floors of the building ceased to operate as a hotel and began operating as small apartments.

The three-story historic building that once served as the Pacific Hotel still stands. Although businesses occupy the main floor today, the upper two floors are empty. The general layouts of hotel rooms are still present in the upper floors. It's difficult to determine from the outside what once occurred within. There are no outwardly visible clues indicating the social or historic impact the building has had in the city, yet its historical importance remains.

The existing owner of the Pacific Hotel building hopes to rejuvenate the upper floors for living quarters and to help preserve its historic past.

20

THE EMPIRE HOTEL

S ome of the last wood buildings to remain standing in the city were located on the south side of East Yakima Avenue, between Front and First Streets. Considered old and eyesores by many in the city, a petition to remove them was presented to city leaders. The petition was denied. The buildings on the south side of Yakima Avenue on this block held several businesses over time. They also served as the northern border of China Town and later Japan Town. Of the wood buildings, two of them that stood midblock were owned by a wealthy woman in the city.

Mary M. (Ditmar) Donald purchased some of the lots as an investment from Patrick Mullins in the early 1900s. Born in Morristown, New Jersey, on May 13, 1878, Mary made her way west when she was about twenty-five years old. She became the second wife of George Donald, twenty years her senior. George was born in Canada and was a railroad employee when he arrived in the Yakima Valley in 1885. Once in the area, he became politically active, a community leader and one of the financial funders of the Yakima Hotel. Both Mary and George were also involved in the Yakima National Bank organization.

Mary's involvement in the bank, along with her purchase of various investment properties, placed her among the most recognized and unusual women of the city. Her purchase of the midblock lots on the south side of East Yakima Avenue soon allowed her to become the owner of one of the largest hotels in the city. Unfortunately, it would take a tragic fire for her hotel to be built.

In 1907, a large fire heavily damaged and destroyed the wood buildings on the south side of East Yakima Avenue between Front Street and the Sloan Building on the southwest corner of East Yakima Avenue and First Street. The buildings on Mary's lots were not spared the devastation. Rather than selling her lots and taking a loss, Mary made the decision to rebuild.

Construction began on Mary's new building soon after the fire. When it was completed in late 1907, it was a three-story brick building that occupied all of her lots. By early 1908, the entire building was filled with businesses. The upper two floors were leased out as a hotel under the proprietorship of

Mary Donald, one-time owner of the Empire Hotel Building.

Mrs. A.E. Daive, who would operate the Empire Hotel from the building. Access to the hotel was through a door located between two of the businesses on the building's street level. With steam heat, new furnishings, electric lights and hot and cold water in every room, the hotel was a modern facility. With a large sign reading "EMPIRE"—with each letter in a circle—attached to the building and hanging far above the sidewalk, the building became the largest on the East Yakima Avenue side of the block.

With the opening of the Empire Hotel, the building once again became an unusual operation. No other building in the city at the time had a woman owner and a different woman running an established hotel from within. The uniqueness of the situation lasted about five years before Daive ended her proprietorship of the Empire Hotel.

Meanwhile, below the hotel, on the main floor of the building, businesses such as Jackson's Barber Shop, the G.S. Garrow Clothing Company, the Giboney Clark Hardware Company, the Yakima Realty & Investment Company and the D.H. Fry Drug Store leased spaces for the first four years. Mary's building was a success, until another fire occurred.

In February 1911, a fire started in the building. The cause was determined to be crossed wires above the Garrow Clothing Company. All hotel rooms were occupied at the time of the fire; luckily, no one was seriously injured. The building suffered significant damages, and merchandise in the buildings

The Empire Hotel Building (right).

were destroyed. After insurance, the total loss for all goods, merchandise and property was estimated to be $28,200. The building was able to be repaired.

It was the second fire on the lots that Mary had experienced since beginning her ownership. Unlike the first fire, when her buildings were lost, she was able to have the damages repaired inside her building. She was so appreciative of the fire department's efforts to save her building that she sent a thank-you note and fifty dollars.

Once repairs were made to the building, business continued as usual for the Empire Hotel, located on the top two floors. On the main floor, various businesses came and went. However, the building was successful for all intents and purposes. That is, of course, until almost a decade later, when a tragedy of a different nature occurred in the hotel.

In April 1920, the guests at the Empire Hotel were woken at four o'clock in the morning and placed under quarantine. It was discovered that several guests in the hotel were suffering from an outbreak of smallpox. Those with the disease were removed from the building; approximately seventy-five other guests and employees had to receive vaccinations.

The following year, the hotel welcomed a new proprietor—one who would not only serve as the longest proprietor in the hotel's history but also one of Japanese heritage who would successfully place the hotel as part of the growing Japan Town.

Bunji Takano was born in Japan on May 10, 1883. In 1907, at about twenty-four years of age, he immigrated to the United States. Three years after arriving, Bunji was a single laborer in Whitefish, Montana. By 1917, he had relocated to Portland, Oregon, and had married Seki Takano. Seki remained in Japan while Bunji worked in Portland.

In 1920, Bunji made his way to Yakima, finding work as a dishwasher and living on South Front Street. The following year, his employment and living location would change. In 1921, he became the new proprietor of the Empire Hotel. A year later, Seki was able to join him in Yakima. The couple lived in room 20, an apartment on the second floor of the hotel. It had a kitchen and living and sleeping areas. Bunji and Seki ran the hotel for twenty-two years while they raised their growing family of four children—one son and three daughters.

Meanwhile, on the main floor, various businesses, like the Empire Clothing Store, occupied the retail areas, while some people rented upstairs hotel rooms as offices, including a Japanese dentist. The hotel not only served as rooms for those visiting the city but also as a more permanent living place for those working elsewhere in the city.

When the evacuation orders for Japanese in the Yakima area occurred, the Takanos lost the Empire Hotel. They were relocated to Heart Mountain, Wyoming, with their neighbors from Japan Town. Bunji and Seki's only son, Tadao (known as Tad), was drafted into the army for World War II. He served while his family was at Heart Mountain Internment Camp.

After leaving Heart Mountain, the Takano family moved to the Chicago area. Like the majority of those from the city, they did not return to Yakima. Tadao joined his family after serving in the military. He later became a professor at the University of Illinois in Chicago and a well-known artist. He passed away in February 2010.

Although they did not move back to Yakima, Seki made a return visit with her daughter Fukiko and son Tadao to see the building from which they once ran the Empire Hotel.

Other businesses opened in the Empire Hotel building, although none lasted as long as the Empire Hotel. Approximately two decades after the Takano family left, the building was demolished to make room for parking. Today, a parking lot and a drive-through bank occupy the location.

21

THE PANAMA HOTEL

Theodore Steiner was born in Pennsylvania about 1853. After traveling west, he arrived in North Yakima in 1885. As the owner of two lots on the south side of East Yakima Avenue between Front and First Streets, Theodore had a two-story building erected. Once completed, he opened the Steiner Hotel on the second floor and the Steiner Restaurant on the main floor. He leased the remaining business space on the main floor to a saloon owner who would eventually own one of the longest-operating saloons in the city.

The Shardlow & Company Saloon opened in the Steiner Hotel building as soon as the structure was finished. Owned by Frank Shardlow, the saloon operated from the Steiner Hotel until approximately 1887, when Frank closed its doors and temporarily relocated to Ellensburg, Washington. (See chapter 2.) With Frank Shardlow's departure, the available space for a saloon in Steiner Hotel was soon filled with another saloon, owned by a different Frank.

Partners Milbern Wills and Frank O'Hara opened the Wills & O'Hara Saloon and Billiard Parlor in the Steiner Hotel in 1888. They advertised as selling fine whiskeys, wines and cigars, as well as having pool and billiards tables. Milbern and Frank's partnership did not last long. By November 1889, Frank had left the venture, leaving Milbern the sole proprietor of the newly named M.G. Wills Saloon.

Two years later, on May 25, 1890, the fire that ravaged the wood buildings on the south side of East Yakima Avenue between Front and First Streets also damaged the Steiner Hotel. Theodore's hotel experienced damages to the cost of $1,500. They were extensive enough that Theodore had to completely rebuild the building. Once construction of the new building was completed, he reopened the Steiner Hotel on the second floor. However, he did not reopen his restaurant. Rather, he invested his money in a Seattle, Washington restaurant.

In 1891, the available space in the new building was filled by one of the city's earliest Chinese-owned restaurants. The Kay & Lucy Restaurant was owned by Ah Kay and Lucy Wong. The two men ran their restaurant at the location for two years; their partnership ended because Lucy returned to China to visit family. Ah stayed in the city and formed a new partnership that would open in a different building, owned by a saloon owner also doing business in Theodore Steiner's building.

After suffering $1,200 in damages from the fire, as well as not having a place to conduct business, Milbern Wills reopened the M.G. Wills Saloon in Theodore's new building. However, Milbern didn't operate his saloon for long. Just two years later, in 1893, he sold his saloon to O.W. Johnson, who renamed it the "Exchange" Saloon. Johnson's saloon would not last long in Steiner's building. He eventually purchased the lot next to Steiner's building and proceeded to construct a new building. When it was completed, he moved his saloon there and leased a space for Ah Kay's new restaurant and partnership.

Two years later, in February 1895, Theodore Steiner vacated his interests in the building and sold it to Peter Herke. Born in Germany to Anthony (Antone) and Gertrude Herke on July 25, 1865, Peter immigrated with his family to America when he was five years old. Although he farmed like his father, he also owned real estate in the city, including a candy store. Building ownership wasn't the only thing that changed on the lot that year; changes to the businesses within the building also occurred.

The lot's first Japanese businessman, K. Thomas Oka, operated a restaurant in the building until 1906. Thomas ran the restaurant for only a brief time, but he would later return to the building and play a more permanent role in its history. In the meantime, the space available after his departure became the home of another Japanese-owned restaurant.

The Grande Restaurant, owned by Noaki Masunaga, opened in Peter Herke's building. Born in Japan, Naoki arrived in the country around 1888. Thirteen years later, his wife, Matsume, who had been living in Japan, joined Noaki in the city.

Changes to the hotel above the restaurant also occurred at this time. The Steiner Hotel was renamed the Yakima Lodging House. Its proprietor was Tom Yong, a Chinese business owner who ran the hotel until 1905. Shortly afterward, the Yakima Hotel was relocated one lot east of the Herke building. A new hotel called the Misui Hotel was opened in the old Steiner Building with Susaka Misui as the proprietor.

Unfortunately, the next business to move into the building would become responsible for changing the entire block. August (Gus) Hammell was born in Germany and arrived in the valley around 1891. Upon arrival, he became engaged in the hops industry. However, in 1906, he opened the August Hammell Cigar Store in the Steiner Building, where he sold not only cigars but also drinks and fireworks.

In August 1907, a fire started behind the August Hammell Cigar Store. Like the previous fire, it devastated the wood buildings along East Yakima Avenue between Front and First Streets. It was the worst fire of the year, with an estimated $50,000 in damages.

Naoki's establishment, the Grande Restaurant, sustained $1,500 in damages and was uninsured. Although uninjured, Noaki was sleeping in the back of his restaurant when the fire started. His cook, who had also been sleeping there, woke him up to alert him about the fire. Twenty people were reported to be sleeping in the lodgings above the restaurant when the building caught on fire. Some accounts reported two deaths; others reported

Looking east on East Yakima Avenue from Front Street, circa 1901. The Herke Brothers Building and future Panama Hotel is the second building on the right.

three. The victims remained unidentified; no next of kin was notified. Sadly, the city buried the unknown victims at Tahoma Cemetery without ceremony. However, some of the Christian Japanese in the city performed a ceremony for the victims so they could rest in peace.

The aftermath of the fire would permanently change the entire appearance of the south side of East Yakima Avenue. With all the wood buildings on the block lining East Yakima Avenue burned or removed due to the fire, the existing business owners relocated or shut their doors permanently. Some building owners began rebuilding using more permanent and fire-resistant materials.

Naoki Masunaga relocated the Grande Restaurant around the corner to South Front Street, where he would also operate a lodging house above it. A decade later, in the 1920s, he was operating a Japanese boardinghouse on South Front Street. Naoki passed away in Wapato, Washington, in 1936.

August Hammell chose to not continue operating a business in the city, opting instead to settle into ranching in the Selah, Washington vicinity. He passed away less than a year after the fire.

Peter Herke, the owner of the building, partnered with his brother Frank to rebuild at the location. They hired a Mr. DeVaux to draw plans for a two-story building measuring 25 feet by 120 feet. Combining forces with the Coffin Brothers, who owned the lot just east of theirs, they decided to have one face across both of their buildings to make them look larger. After the plans were put in place, the Herke Brothers hired C.H. Bruenn to construct their new building.

Construction started on the Herke Brothers Building in September 1907. It took twenty-eight men to erect the building—fourteen carpenters, five brick workers, six tenders and an elevator boy. The men even worked on the building on Thanksgiving Day—not because they didn't honor the holiday, but they hadn't received an official proclamation from the governor of Washington State proclaiming the day to be Thanksgiving.

When the Herke Brothers' new building was completed in April 1908, it occupied both of their lots. The upstairs was leased out as the Natches Lodging House to Mr. and Mrs. J.J. Schreiber. Meanwhile, on the main floor, the Red Apple Café opened. The café functioned from this location for years, with various Chinese restaurant owners as proprietors. Other businesses occupied the east side of the main floor of the building over time.

One of the rooms in the upstairs lodging house belonged to the Herke Brothers' father, Anthony (Antone) Herke. Anthony was born in Germany on October 9, 1836, immigrating to the country with his wife, Gertrude,

Installation of tracks at East Yakima Avenue and Front Street, 1908. The Herke Brothers Building (later known as the Panama Hotel) is the two-story white building on the right.

and children in 1870. The family arrived in New York and then made their way west to California, north to Oregon and, eventually, farther north to the Yakima Valley. Anthony, considered one of the early pioneers in the area, had homesteaded 160 acres in the Ahtanum area around 1871.

Anthony and Gertrude had ten children together, six of whom survived to adulthood. He and his descendants purchased large amounts of property throughout the valley, including in the Parker area. It was in this area that Anthony was farming when he contracted malaria. With his health deteriorating, he took a room in the Herke Brothers' building. In December 1908, Anthony Herke passed away in the lodging house, surrounded by family.

The Herke Brothers continued to own the building after their father's death, with other businesses leasing out space. The Natches Lodging House upstairs was still under the Schreibers' care until 1911. After their departure, the hotel name would change under the direction of the next proprietor. Two business owners in the hotel would also be Japanese, making the building a key player in the expanding Japan Town of the city.

In 1912, the hotel on the upper floors of the Herke Brothers building became the Panama Hotel under the ownership of Joe Sakimura. He was born in Japan in approximately 1888. For the first five years as the proprietor of the hotel, he was single. He then traveled to Seattle, Washington, and married Fuyo Saito. Fuyo was also born in Japan and had come to America to marry Joe. After being united in marriage at the Seattle Buddhist Church on November 23, 1916, the couple returned to North Yakima and continued to run the Panama Hotel for three more years. In 1919, they left the hotel business and opened the Tokio Tea Parlor on South First Street.

At about the same time that Joe Sakimura became the proprietor of the Panama Hotel, another Japanese man, also named Joe, opened a business from within the hotel. Joe Kimura rented a room in the hotel and started a Japanese employment agency. Born in Japan on October 28, 1890, Joe arrived in America in 1908 or 1909 and was running his agency within a few years of his arrival. In 1918, his wife, Yoshi Iwase, who had remained in Japan, joined him in the city. Joe Kimura's employment agency closed in the Panama Hotel a few years before Joe Sakimura stopped running the hotel. However, he continued playing an active role in the Japanese community of the valley.

In 1922, the secretary of the interior, A.B. Fall, decided to deny the leasing of Indian reservation land to non-immigrants. Joe Kimura actively attended Japanese Association of Yakima County meetings and stressed the importance of the Japanese in the valley learning English. He became one of the driving forces in providing English-language classes.

He also wasn't done running a business in the city. Between 1928 and 1937, Joe Kimura owned and operated the Togo Clothing Company, located just one lot west of the Panama Hotel. In 1935, he was also running a store in the Annex Building, one building south of the Pacific Hotel. All the while, he maintained his active role in the Japanese community until his death on August 14, 1939.

With the departure of Joe Sakimura and Joe Kimura from the building, an opportunity for a former occupant to return arose. K. Thomas Oka, owner of one of the former restaurants at the site, returned to do business in the building. This time, he became the co-owner of the Panama Hotel with J. Nojiri. The partnership ended within two years; Thomas remained as the sole proprietor of the hotel until 1926.

By 1929, the hotel would finally get its longest proprietor. Peter K. Fujii was born in Japan and arrived in the country in 1902. Little is known about Peter with the exception that, in 1923, he was living at the Empire Hotel.

While residing in the hotel, he worked as a cook at the Lions Café on South Front Street. In 1927, at the approximate age of thirty-seven, Peter took over sole proprietorship of the Panama Hotel. The following year, he was also the owner of the Lions Café on South Front Street. Although his ownership of the café was brief, he served as the Panama Hotel proprietor until the evacuation of the Japanese from the city in 1942.

After the evacuation, the Panama Hotel Building remained standing. Various businesses occupied the main floor. Eventually, along with the other buildings located on the south side of East Yakima Avenue on the block, the Panama Hotel building was demolished. Today, a drive-through bank and a parking lot are located at the approximate site.

PART V

THE OPIUM TUNNELS AND DENS

The import, sale and use of opium on the West Coast escalated in the 1880s. To eliminate the opium issue, political and municipal leaders began introducing laws to stop its import, while law enforcement began making arrests of those selling and using the drug. North Yakima was no different.

Within ten years of North Yakima becoming a city, it was experiencing issues with the import, sale and use of opium. The problem occurred throughout the city, but the area known by locals as China Town was the only one being routinely reported as having opium-related issues.

In 1893, the North Yakima Police Department patrolled China Town and began raiding buildings and businesses thought to have opium sales or use. Most accounts of opium-related busts involved finding only opium paraphernalia. However, there were busts involving people smoking opium. Once discovered, the police would typically destroy the paraphernalia, not keeping it for evidence, and arrest those smoking it. It is an odd procedure considering today's standards for evidence.

A year later, the smoking of opium wasn't the only problem law enforcement was experiencing when it came to ridding the city of the drug. A large opium-smuggling operation was discovered. The drug was smuggled into the country and then brought to North Yakima, where it was divided up and distributed throughout the Northwest. The smuggling operation did not help lessen the impact of the drug on the city, nor did the continual use of the drug by those in the city.

In 1908, frequent opium busts were occurring, and city leaders had finally had enough. They began taking extreme measures to eliminate not only the drug from the city but also those they felt were associated with it. One action taken was to order business owners suspected of being involved to leave the city. The first known removal of people from the city occurred when City Councilman Andrew Shaw signed a resolution ordering the chief of police to notify owners of several businesses to leave within three days or face arrest. He also instructed the chief to tell the Chinese citizens even suspected of frequenting opium dens to stay in China Town and off the other streets of the city.

The resolution did little to deter the use of opium, but it did give the chief of police more authority to conduct more raids, which is exactly what he proceeded to do. In the summer of 1908, opium busts were occurring with more frequency. One such raid occurred on South Front Street near East Walnut. Arrests of Chinese were made, and two opium pipes were obtained. Not long afterward, another bust occurred on South Front Street between East Chestnut and East Walnut, resulting in the arrest of six Chinese and the seizure of opium, pipes and other paraphernalia. Those arrested in the raid were given a twenty-five-dollar bail and set free with a trial awaiting them. It was at their trial that the court was questioned regarding the legality of arresting people for the smoking of opium.

The defense attorney hired for the six Chinamen was Henry J. Snively, one of the most prominent attorneys in the city. During the trial, Snively questioned the city's ordinance prohibiting the smoking of opium. Washington State laws prohibiting the smoking of opium at the time were not applicable to third-class cities unless the state granted it. (Cities at the time were ranked based on population. North Yakima was a third-class city at that time.) In other words, North Yakima didn't have the authority to contradict the state law. Although the city's attorney agreed that the city didn't have the power to regulate the smoking of opium, he argued in court that it did have the right to exercise liberal police power. The case was the first time the city's power to arrest people for smoking opium was questioned.

Regardless of the legality, it didn't stop officers from arresting those found in opium dens. In fact, the following year, the Yakima County Sheriff's Department collaborated with the North Yakima Police Department in opium raids within the city. The combination of the two forces led to several raids, one of which resulted in the arrest of non-Chinese citizens.

On a February day in 1909, members of the North Yakima Police Department and the Yakima County Sherriff's Department raided five opium dens in the city. It was the biggest raid reported in the city's history and resulted in twenty Chinese and two Caucasian men being arrested, as well as opium and paraphernalia seized.

The locations of the dens raided that day included a store and Chinese lodging houses. More notable, however, were the various underground caves raided. Reports of the cave raids mentioned that each cave had two exits with bars and were connected to small underground passages that ran throughout China Town. Both the caves and tunnels were reported as being guarded, but not well. They were also noted as being the homes to several Chinese men. A Chinese woman was also found within the network of dens and tunnels, but she managed to escape.

Law enforcement and city officials were now faced with the knowledge that it wasn't only the Chinese frequenting opium-smoking facilities. Ironically, the two white men arrested were given a twenty-five-dollar fine for smoking opium, but they forfeited their bail and left the city. Of the twenty Chinese arrested that morning, nineteen were charged with smoking opium. Each was fined twenty-five dollars.

Opium-related issues occurring within dens and tunnels continued in the city, but after the 1908 and 1909 raids, it was reported less frequently. During Prohibition, the tunnels were thought to be used for bootlegging. Later, gambling was also taking place underground. As recently as the 1970s, people in the city have reported witnessing those running from the law, including prostitutes and others, entering the old opium tunnels and dens in China Town to escape authorities.

The exact networking of the opium tunnels connecting the dens is unknown today, and most reported entrances have been sealed off. They are also often confused with other tunnel networks in the city that were placed for steam-heating purposes. Unlike the steam tunnels installed at other places in the city, the opium tunnels were reported as being much smaller and made of dirt and other materials. They were a separate system from others in the city.

Today, only one known entry to the opium tunnels and dens within China Town is thought to exist. It is unknown if the entry allows passage to the tunnel system and the closed dens. Other entries are thought to have been sealed off decades ago.

Specific reported locations of the entries to the China Town opium dens and tunnels discussed in this chapter were not identified for a reason. Entries to the dens and tunnels—open and closed—located within remaining buildings are on private property. Other reported entries lay under parking lots. Identifying their locations when underground tunnels are of social interest could be considered detrimental to existing property owners. Furthermore, they've been underground for more than a century, so it is not known if they are safe for passage.

BIBLIOGRAPHY

Aberdeen (WA) Herald. "Forbids Music in Saloons." June 18, 1906.

Anaheim Libraries Virtual Branch. "First Generation." https://www.anaheim.net/2686/anaheim.net/First-Generation.

———. "Frank C. Hirahara's Legacy Is Opening the Door for Others to Tell Their Stories." https://www.anaheim.net/2686/First-Generation.

———. "Second Generation." https://www.anaheim.net/2686/anaheim.net/Second-Generation.

Ayer, Tammy. "Ghosts of Japan Town, Few Buildings Remain of Once-Vibrant Yakima Community." *Yakima Herald-Republic*. April 12, 2017.

———. "Items from Yakima Father and Son Incarcerated at Heart Mountain, Wyo., Part of Smithsonian Exhibition." *Yakima Herald-Republic*. February 23, 2017.

———. "Little Remains of Yakima's Once-Vibrant Japan Town." *Yakima Herald-Republic*. June 12, 2017.

———. "Yakima's Japan Town No Longer There, but Rich History Remains." *Yakima Herald-Republic*, February 19, 2017.

Berger, Knute. "Meet Nell Pickerell, Transgender At-risk Youth of Yesteryear." Crosscut.com, June 30, 2014. crosscut.com/2014/06/nell-pickerell-transgender-youth-knute-berger.

Brown, Lois, Pat Brown, Bryan Brown, Greta Brown, Theo Mays and Nancy K. Lindsey. *100 Years, 100 Women 1889–1989, Yakima County Washington*. Edited by Theo Mays. Yakima, WA: Print Masters, 1989.

Butte Daily Post. "Robbed the Gamblers." January 23, 1901.

BIBLIOGRAPHY

Chin, Curtis S. "Commentary: Add a Touch of History and Heritage to Thanksgiving." *Northwest Asian Weekly*. www.nwasianweekly.com/2013.

Coeur d'Alene (ID) Press. "Fight on Saloons at Yakima, Wash.." October 6, 1909.

East Oregonian (Pendleton, OR). "Big Depot for Yakima." August 13, 1908.

———. "Brewery at North Yakima." November 28, 1904.

———. "Drive Elephants Away." March 17, 1908.

———. "Eight Yakima Saloons May Go." November 26, 1908.

———. "Floto Show Was Good." October 2, 1905.

———. "Indian Whisky Problem at Yakima." September 14, 1906.

———. "Mayor for Yakima Beer." October 20, 1911.

———. "North Yakima Needs a Jail." September 15, 1905.

———. "Pastor and Brewer See City Together." January 19, 1910.

———. "Raid Yakima Dens, 22 in Net." February 9, 1909.

Ellensburg Dawn. "New Brewery at Yakima." December 1, 1904.

Evening Statesman (Walla Walla, WA). "Circus Roustabout Dies." June 2, 1906.

———. "Hotel Partners Disagree." September 19, 1903.

———. "Japanese to Celebrate." July 3, 1909.

———. "North Yakima Jail Crowded." May 18, 1904.

———. "North Yakima Jail Filthy." March 8, 1909.

———. "Prohibition Waves Stops Work on a Brewery." February 19, 1908.

———. "Raid Chinese Gambling Joint." August 01, 1909.

———. "Restaurant Keeper Disobey Police." February 21, 1908.

———. "To Veto Saloon Ordinance." November 12, 1906.

———. "Yakima Has a 'Dry' Sunday." May 24, 1905.

Gaylord, Mary. *Eastern Washington's Past Chinese & Other Pioneers, 1860–1910. A Self Guided Auto Tour to the State's Diverse Heritage.* Portland, OR: Forest Service USDA, 1993.

Gazette-Times (Heppner, OR). "Breweries Will Change to Canneries." November 19, 1914.

Great Falls (MT) Daily Tribune. "Yakima Smallpox Causes All in Hotel to Be Vaccinated." April 7, 1920.

Heuterman, Thomas H. *The Burning Horse: The Japanese-American Experience in the Yakima Valley, 1920–1942.* Cheney: Eastern Washington University Press, 1995.

Hildebrand, Lorraine Barker. "Straw Hats, Sandals and Steel: The Chinese in Washington State." *The Washington State American Revolution Bicentennial Commission,* 1977. Tacoma.

Hirahara, Patti. "The Story of One of the Last Picture Brides in the United States." AsAmNews, October 7, 2014. https://asamnews.com.

An Illustrated History of Klickitat, Yakima and Kittitas Counties; With an Outline of the Early History of the State of Washington. Chicago: Interstate Publishing Company, 1904.

Jackson, Gary L., ed. "The Length of Their Shadows." Volume 2 of *Remembering Yakima by Those Who Were There*. Yakima, WA: Golden West Publishing, 1975.

———, ed. "Remembering the Yakima Valley." Volume 6 of *Remembering Yakima by Those Who Were There*. Yakima, WA: Golden West Publishing, 1975.

———, ed. "Remembering Yakima by Those Who Were There, Chin-On…He Brought a Bit of Old World China to Yakima." *Yakima Valley Sun*. Yakima, WA: Golden West, December 11, 1975.

———, ed. "Yakima's Historical Citizens." Volume 5 of *Remembering Yakima by Those Who Were There*. Yakima, WA: Golden West Publishing, 1975.

———, ed. "Yakima's Past." Volume 3 of *Remembering Yakima by Those Who Were There*. Yakima, WA: Golden West Publishing, 1975.

Janovich, Adriana. "The Railroad Influence." Yakima —The Beginning. April 22, 2010. http://yakimathebeginning.com/2010/04/the-railroad-influence.

Kennewick (WA) Courier. "North Coast Condemns." September 18, 1908.

Letizia, Nella. "Family Photos Inspire Events About Japanese Internment." WSU Libraries, October 8, 2014, Washington State University. https://news.wsu.edu.

Lewiston (ID) Evening Teller. "Boost Brewery Assessment." August 7, 1908.

———. "City's Power Questioned." October 28, 1908.

———. "Discharge Yakima Police Chief." October 21, 1908.

———. "Investigate Police Department." October 7, 1908.

———. "Yakima Saloons in Balance." August 13, 1908.

———. "Yakima Saloons to Stay." August 19, 1908.

Lyman, William Denison. *History of the Yakima Valley, Washington; Comprising Yakima, Kittitas, and Benton Counties*. Chicago: S.J. Clarke, 1919.

Martin, George M., Paul Schafer, and William E. Scofield. *Yakima: A Centennial Reflection, 1885–1985*. A Publication of the Yakima Centennial Commission, Pat Brown, Editorial Consultant. Yakima, WA: Shields Bag and Publishing, January 1, 1985, 10–36.

Muir, Pat. "Did Chinese Workers Build Secret Passageways Under Yakima?" From *Discover Yakima Valley*. 2012 Annual. http://www.discoveryakimavalley.com.

Neiwert, David A. *Strawberry Days, How Internment Destroyed a Japanese American Community*. New York: St. Martin's Press, 2005.

Oldham, Kit. "Northern Pacific Railroad Reaches Yakima City, Where It Declines to Build a Station, on December 17, 1884." February 18, 2003. HistoryLink.org. http://www.historylink.org/File/5237.

Relander, Click, and George M. Martin. "Yakima Washington Jubilee, 1885–1960." Yakima, WA: Yakima Diamond Jubilee and Franklin Press, 1960.

Seattle Post-Intelligencer. "State Industrial Convention." July 18, 1891.

———. "Yakima Jail Delivery." September 6, 1900.

Seattle Star. "Nell Pickerell Dead." December 28, 1922.

————. "Nell Pickerell May Die of Wounds." September 27, 1916.

————. "New Fire Department." May 17, 1904.

Spokane Press. "Brewer and Pastor Travel Together on Booze Investigation." January 30, 1910.

————. "Christianized Chinese Buys His Wife." September 4, 1908.

————. "Circus Causes Revolution." June 4, 1908.

————. "Japs and Chinese in Hashery Trust." February 24, 1908.

————. "To Close Yakima Saloons." January 2, 1908.

Statesman Journal (Salem, OR). "Yakima Hotel Man Is Wounded by Partner." September 3, 1921.

Troianello, Craig. "Life in the Valley: Past Is Prologue." Yakima: The Beginning. April 22, 2010. https://www.yakimathebeginning.com.

United States Department of the Interior, letter to Mr. Guy Robinson from Mr. Murray E. Stebbins, dated May 23, 1945.

United States Department of the Interior War Relocation Authority, letter to Mr. Guy Robinson from Mr. Murray E. Stebbins, dated June 15, 1945.

Washington Standard. "Local Brewery to Keep On Running." November 13, 1914.

Wenatchee Daily World. "Attach the Circus Elephant." May 27, 1907.

————. "Yakima Votes Wet; 271 Majority." December 31, 1909.

Yakima Herald. "Add Two Stories to Tieton Hotel." September 15, 1909.

————. "Among the Old Timers." January 3, 1901.

————. Anthony Herke, Pioneer, Dead." December 30, 1908.

————. "Anti-Saloon Vote Dec. 20." October 20, 1909.

————. "August Hammel." June 10, 1908.

————. "Band Concert." August 22, 1901.

————. "Black Stockings." May 15, 1907.

————. "A Butte Millionaire Buys Yakima Property." August 17, 1904.

————. "Chin Chan Leaves for China." January 15, 1908.

————. "Chinks and Booze." April 22, 1908.

————. "City Jail Is a Vile Hole." March 16, 1910.

————. "City's Wise Move." September 11, 1907.

————. "Commemorate Birthday." February 19, 1908.

————. "Corner Stone Laid." September 6, 1905.

————. "Death Takes Old Settlers." December 29, 1909.

————. "DOG SAVES $1,000." July 31, 1907.

————. "A Double Marriage." May 21, 1891.

————. "Draw Line on Avenue Bars." September 8, 1909.

————. "Early Morning Fire in Hotel Empire Causes Heavy Damage to Retail Firms." February 15, 1911.

————. "Fine Fruit in Windows." September 30, 1908.

————. "The Fire Department." May 3, 1905.

————. "Flee from Parents." August 19, 1908.

————. "Free of Charge." February 28, 1901.

————. "Gathered about Home." November 9, 1899.

————. "Hop Smokers Draw Fines." February 10, 1909.

————. "Informs City Clerk Brooker that He Will Not Be in Field for Fifth Ward Place." October 21, 1908.

————. "Japanese Baby Honored." October 24, 1906.

————. "Japanese Travels to See His Parents." December 14, 1910. Image 9, Library of Congress Digital Archives.

————. "Last Brick Laid on Hotel Michigan." November 22, 1911.

————. "Mailloux Wins the Fruit Prize." September 25, 1907.

————. "Make Big Howl." March 18, 1908.

————. "Make First Arrest Under Ordinance Covering Licenses." April 15, 1908.

————. "Montana Hotel to Reopen." September 11, 1912.

————. "Mrs. Donald Pays $40,000 for Corner." May 3, 1911.

————. "Musicians Form Permanent Union." July 31, 1907.

————. "Must Leave Town." May 6, 1908.

————. "Nell Canned Again." March 10, 1909.

————. "New Buildings." September 18, 1907.

————. "New Hotel." April 8, 1908.

————. "Northern Pacific Depot Filthy Place for the People." April 1, 1908.

————. "Northwest Painters Have Conference in North Yakima." September 18, 1907, 3.

————. "North Yakima a Depot." March 1, 1894.

————. "North Yakima Expansion." December 28, 1899.

————. "North Yakima's Big Fire." May 29, 1890.

————. "Notorious Nell Pickerell Lands in Yakima Jail." March 18, 1908.

————. "Pioneer Cigar Man Sells." March 11, 1908.

————. "Police Force Is Cut in Two." September 6, 1907.

————. "Raids Opium Joint." May 6, 1908.

————. "Reports Are Current that There Will Be a Transfer of Business of Large House." October 21, 1908.

————. "Restaurant Keepers Found Not Guilty." April 22, 1908.

————. "The Richelieu." August 23, 1894. Newspaper.com.

————. "Sam Chong and Wong Hop Are in Toils of Law." April 15, 1908.

———. "Sam Chong Fined in Restaurant Box Case." May 5, 1909.

———. "Schott Co. Store Robbed." September 26, 1901.

———. "Shoots at Fleeing Prisoner on Street." November 22, 1911.

———. "Six Chinese in Opium Den." August 26, 1908.

———. "State Wants Liquor Money." April 20, 1910.

———. "Substantial Thanks to Fire Department." February 22, 1911.

———. "Tax and the Saloons." April 15, 1908.

———. "Third Story for Pacific." June 27, 1906.

———. "Three Japanese Registered Here." January 26, 1910.

———. "To Close Yakima Saloons." January 8, 1908.

———. "To Enforce Screen Law." June 2, 1909.

———. "To Fight Eagles, Saloon Men Will Combat Club Room." April 1, 1908.

———. "A Touching Memorial." August 21, 1907.

———. "Turnell Loses Pacific Hotel." October 28, 1908.

———. "Twenty Chinks and Two Whites Caught in Raid." February 10, 1909.

———. "Two Story Building." September 4, 1907.

———. "'Typewriter' Ordinance Passed over Mayor's Veto." February 8, 1905.

———. "Union Men to Have Eight Hour Whistle." July 17, 1907.

———. "Will Attract Attention." July 5, 1905.

———. "Will Stop Sales." June 17, 1908.

———. "Work Progresses." December 4, 1907.

———. "Yakima Is Closed." January 8, 1908.

———. "Yakima the Worst." August 7, 1907.

Yakima Valley Museum. "Land of Joy and Sorrow: Japanese Pioneers of the Yakima Valley" (exhibit). http://yakimavalleymuseum.org.

INDEX

ABOUT THE AUTHOR

E llen Allmendinger lives in Yakima, Washington, with her husband and son, where she leads historical walking tours of downtown Yakima, Tahoma Cemetery and other local vicinities. Her tours cover the history of Yakima, historic buildings, businesses, events and people of the city. Areas covered on her downtown Yakima tours include the Historic Block, Japan Town and China Town. She also assists with historical research for various public and private organizations.

As a public speaker, Ellen has given several presentations and has served on panels regarding Yakima Valley history for various public and private events, conferences, organizations, clubs and community gatherings.

She also assists with historical research for various public and private organizations.

Visit us at
www.historypress.com